Magical
Meaningful
Memorable

RECIPES, HOW-TO'S
AND INSPIRATION

ANDY GOLDFARB

Mission

Breaking Matzo's mission is to make Jewish Home Holidays even more magical, meaningful and memorable by sharing ideas about Food, Fun and Philosophy. All of my ideas are inspired by the Torah, my heart or taught by my mom and other family members. Our family is filled with rabbis, cooks and passionate learners. I have enjoyed these traditions as a child and with my children, brothers, family and friends my entire life. I am so heartened that the content of Breaking Matzo is enjoyed by such a diverse community of Jews, Christians and Muslims from all over the world. It is beautiful to see so much interest in Judaism, the Torah and the Jewish Home Holidays traditions. Our goal is to stimulate the mind, touch the heart and uplift the soul. Breaking Matzo is so fortunate to have such an engaged, compassionate and positive community. I feel so grateful to be the founder of Breaking Matzo which has been a catalyst for so much sharing and caring.

You can follow Breaking Matzo on Facebook, Instagram, YouTube, Pinterest and BreakingMatzo.com.

Scan to visit BreakingMatzo.com

Contents

Introduction 11

Passover 12

Shavuot 72

Succot 78

Hanukkah 124

Shabbat..................... 170

Fun Projects 212

Additional Videos 224

Recipe Index................ 230

For Mom

I would like to dedicate this book to my mom, Myra Yellin Goldfarb Outwater (of Blessed Memory, 7/11/42-11/2/15) or Nana as my children affectionately called her. My mom taught me so many recipes and inspired my love of cooking. My favorite memories of my mom centered on preparing for and celebrating Jewish holidays — cooking latkes for Hanukkah, building our succah, and my favorite food memory — my mom's Chocolate Matzo Mousse Cake. My brothers and I always fought over who got to lick the spatula with the leftover chocolate mousse. My mom always made her Chocolate Matzo Mousse Cake with my daughters, Caroline and Lucy, for Passover. We continue to make it each Passover to remember Nana.

Mom, you have forever inspired me with your indefatigable energy, relentless positivity, infectious enthusiasm and contagious curiosity. I love you so much!

Love, Andy

Introduction

"Magical, Meaningful, Memorable" is brought to you by Andy Goldfarb, founder of Breaking Matzo, an inspirational lifestyle blog that celebrates Jewish Home Holidays as well as educates and inspires Jews, Christians and Muslims on the Food, Fun and Philosophy of Passover, Hanukkah, Succot and Shabbat. In this book, you'll find a range of Kosher and Kosher for Passover recipes from classics such as Matzo Ball Soup and Potato Latkes to a potpourri of nine international Charoset recipes, Chocolate Matzo Mousse Cake and Apple Rose Pastries. Also included are Fun DIY projects to involve young children in preparing for holidays such as creating a DIY Seder Plate for Passover. You will also find educational content and spiritual discussion questions to stimulate lively and meaningful dinner discussions during your holiday celebrations. You can learn even more about the recipes and holidays by scanning QR codes (example below) in this book to launch companion videos and content designed to supplement the content. I fervently hope that this book helps make your Jewish Home Holiday celebrations even more magical, meaningful and memorable!

Scan for BreakingMatzo.com

Passover

CHAROSETS & CONDIMENTS
Classic Ashkenazi Charoset
Chinese Charoset
Indian Charoset
Iraqi Charoset
Italian Charoset
Moroccan Charoset
Piedmontese Charoset
Spanish Charoset

Yemenite Charoset
Etrog Marmalade

APPETIZERS & SIDES
Charoset Chicken Salad
Shang and Emma's Tzimmes

ENTREES
"Lucky" Matzo Balls with
Schmaltz and Gribenes

Passover celebrates the Exodus journey from slavery in Egypt to wandering in the wilderness and finally reaching freedom in the Promised Land. Each year, we gather our family and friends around the Seder table to retell this meaningful story by reading the Haggadah (prayer book). In the center of our table, as in every Jewish home, is the Seder Plate which represents the major themes of the Passover story.

During Passover, we give up all leavened products, eating matzo which is unleavened instead of "chametz" (leavened bread). Giving up chametz and eating matzo helps us focus on the basics in our lives and reflect on our ongoing journeys from slavery to freedom. Matzo is a key ingredient we get creative with during this holiday: Matzo Ball Soup, Chocolate Matzo Mousse Cake and Chocolate Covered Matzo to name a few.

Golden Chicken Soup
Grandma Boody's Brisket
Freedom Lamb
Matzo Brei

DESSERTS
Rose Water Almond Cookies
Chocolate Matzo Mousse Cake
Chocolate Covered Matzo
Coconut Cheesecake with Candied Lemon Curls

BEVERAGE
Indian-Jewish Sangria

These recipes are all kosher for Passover.

V = Vegan
GF = Gluten Free

PASSOVER 13

Charoset

Charoset is a food of slavery, representing the mortar for the bricks made by the Hebrew slaves. Why is it sweet? Sometimes what we are building can seem sweet even though we are serving a false god.

Charoset can also help explain the tale of the Jewish Diaspora. Wherever Jews landed, they used local ingredients for their Charoset. The recipe changed but the tradition of representing the bricks and mortar of the Hebrew enslavement in Egypt did not.

My goal is to celebrate the Jewish Diaspora. I want all nine varieties of Charoset to represent a universal message that all of the people of the world, despite different flavors, share the common quest to escape from modern day slavery and return to our Promised Land.

Classic Ashkenazi Charoset
—

This is a traditional Ashkenazi charoset. Its signature ingredients are apples, walnuts, cinnamon, honey and sweet Manischewitz wine. We make this easy charoset with the young kids during our cocktail hour before we start our Seder. Kids love getting involved.

Makes approximately 4 cups

INGREDIENTS

2 medium-sized apples

½ cup walnuts, chopped

1 tsp cinnamon

2 tsp sweet red Kosher wine, such as Manischewitz

1 tbsp sugar or honey or to taste

INSTRUCTIONS

Peel, core and finely chop or grate the apple

Mix with the rest of the ingredients in a bowl and serve

Chinese Charoset

Common ingredients in Chinese cuisine are highlighted in this version of charoset: soy sauce, pine nuts and honey. In contrast with most charoset recipes, this one is slightly savory.

I lived in Japan and worked for Kikkoman Soy Sauce. I also traveled in China and studied the Fugu Plan, a Japanese rescue plan to save Jews from the Nazis by settling them in Shanghai during World War II. This Charoset recipe creates a connection between the wandering Jews of China and the Passover story.

Makes approximately 6 cups

INGREDIENTS

½ pound of dates (about 1½ cups, finely chopped)

4 apples (finely chopped)

½ cup pine nuts

3 tbsp soy sauce (you can use gluten-free) Coconut Aminos or Bragg's Liquid Aminos can be substituted for soy sauce for Passover

4 tbsp honey

juice of 1 orange

INSTRUCTIONS

Heat all ingredients in a saucepan until soft and smooth (about 5 minutes)

Scan for video

Indian Charoset

V, GF

I wanted to highlight the flavors of the Jewish Experience in India. Did you know that Jews have lived in India for over 2,800 years and were the first foreign religious group to enter the country?

It is not surprising that the combination of Indian flavors and Jewish tradition creates such a delicious and unique recipe. We hope that you will love the combination of flavors of the mango, papaya and cashews along with aromatic Indian spices.

Makes approximately 3 cups

INGREDIENTS

1 large papaya (or 2 small), peeled, seeded & finely chopped

1 cup dried mango, diced

¾ cup whole raw cashews

juice of 1 lemon

½ tsp freshly grated peeled ginger

¼ tsp cinnamon

⅛ tsp each ground cloves & cardamom

INSTRUCTIONS

Mix all ingredients together and serve

Recommend making fresh but you can make it a day ahead and refrigerate. If you would like to tailor your recipe, you can add ground date paste to symbolize the mortar the slaves used to build the walls during their slavery in Egypt. For another type of Indian Charoset, grind the ingredients into a paste which is part of the recipe tradition of the Bene Israel Indian Jews

Iraqi Charoset

V, GF

In our pursuit of discovering Jewish recipes from around the world, we came across this simple Iraqi Charoset for Passover — just pure date syrup and chopped almonds.

Yield: 1 lb of dates makes approximately ½-¾ cup date syrup

INGREDIENTS

2-½ lbs dates (or 1-½ cups store bought date syrup)

handful of pecans, roughly chopped

INSTRUCTIONS

Pit and halve dates

Place in a saucepan and cover with water. Bring to a boil then lower heat and simmer for 20 minutes

Strain and return dates to the pan and cover with water again, this time ensuring there's about an inch more of water. Bring to a boil then lower heat and simmer covered for 2 hours, checking occasionally to ensure there's still enough water in the pan

Strain dates and squeeze liquid through a nut milk bag into a bowl. Squeeze really hard to ensure you have all that precious juice out

Put the juice back on the stove in a sauce pan and reduce until it becomes a thick syrup. Takes about 25-30 minutes. Let cool

Pour date syrup in a small bowl and top with chopped pecans. Serve with matzo crackers

NOTES

You can store date syrup in a glass container in the refrigerator for weeks.

PASSOVER

Italian Charoset

V, GF

Pine nuts, pears and almonds evoke the flavors and textures of Italian sweet and savory food. If a Jewish family, living in Piedmont, were making a locally based charoset, they would find all the ingredients here. It's a beautiful dish, and like many, my family loves Italian cooking.

Makes approximately 7 cups

INGREDIENTS

3 apples, cored, peeled & chopped

2 pears, cored, peeled & chopped

¾ cup yellow raisins or sultanas

1 cup prunes, pitted & finely chopped

1⅓ cups dates, pitted & chopped

2 cups sweet red Kosher wine, such as Manischewitz

⅓ cup pine nuts

⅔ cup almonds, finely chopped

½ cup sugar or honey

1 tsp cinnamon

½ tsp ground ginger

INSTRUCTIONS

Cut the pears and apples into small pieces

Put all the ingredients in a saucepan and cook on low heat, stirring occasionally, for about 20-30 minutes, until the fruits are very soft, adding a little water if it becomes too dry

VARIATION

Other possible additions: chopped lemon or candied orange peel, walnuts, pistachios, dried figs, orange or lemon juice, ginger, nutmeg and cloves.

History:

The history of the Jews in Italy spans more than 2,000 years. The Jewish presence in Italy dates to the pre-Christian Roman period. Despite periods of extreme persecutions and expulsions from parts from time to time, the Italian Jewish community has always been resilient and plays an important role in Italian culture.

The first documented Jews in Italy were the ambassadors sent to Rome by Judah Maccabee in 161 BCE. When the Jews were expelled from Spain in 1492, many of them found refuge in Italy, where they were given protection by King Ferdinand I of Naples.

The Venetian Ghetto was the area of Venice in which Jews were compelled to live under the Venetian Republic. It is from its name in Italian ("ghetto"), that the English word "ghetto" is derived. In the Venetian language it was named "ghèto." The Venetian Ghetto (incidentally, the first ghetto) was instituted in 1516.

Moroccan Charoset

Dates, walnuts and cloves give this charoset its deep color and thick consistency. We love the delicious tangy flavor and smooth texture. It is so rich with the flavor of the dates and cloves. This may be our favorite charoset. Make extra for wonderful leftovers after the Seder!

Makes approximately 3 cups

INGREDIENTS

1 lb dates, pitted & chopped (about 3 cups)

1½ cups sweet red Kosher wine, such as Manischewitz

1 tsp ground cinnamon

½ tsp ground cloves

1 cup walnuts, coarsely chopped

INSTRUCTIONS

Put the dates in a pan with the wine, cinnamon and cloves then simmer, stirring occasionally, until you have a soft paste (about 5 minutes). Pulse in a food processor if you want a smoother texture

Let it cool and stir in the walnuts

VARIATION

A Libyan version is flavored with ground ginger, nutmeg and cloves: ¼ tsp of each.

History:

Moroccan Jews are the descendants of an ancient Jewish Community. Jews in Morocco date back to the earliest reaches of Morocco's history. Jews in the Roman Empire pre-dated Christ, and those Jews most likely migrated along the Mediterranean into what is now Morocco. They created communities and converted natives to Judaism. In the eighth century, Arab armies built up an empire that included both Morocco and Spain. Towards the end of the eighth century, Idriss I created the first Muslim state in the central and western areas of Morocco. With Idriss I fighting and forcing conversions, Jews and Christians fled to Moroccan regions not under his domain. In the early ninth century, Idriss I's son, Idriss II, founded Fez. He invited the Jews to live alongside the Arabs in Fez. Although the Jewish community remained considerably restricted, Fez did offer opportunities for prosperity. Jews remained there peacefully for the ninth and tenth centuries.

Fast Forward to the 1900s. After the killings of a few Europeans in Casablanca and Marrakesh in 1907, the French found an excuse for an invasion of Morocco, occupying Casablanca and pillaging the mellah. The French and Spanish governments both took significant sections of Morocco from 1907-1912, making Tangier an international zone. By 1941, the Vichy government of France imposed oppressive laws upon Moroccan Jews, setting quotas on doctors, lawyers, and students, forcing many Jews into mellahs. The Sultan, Mohammed V, announced his opposition to the oppressive laws and asked Muslims not to hurt the Jews, saying they were loyal subjects. The Sultan famously and courageously said "There are no Jews in Morocco," and declared "There are only Moroccan subjects." "I absolutely do not approve of the new anti-Semitic laws and I refuse to associate myself with a measure I disagree with," he told the French officials. "I reiterate as I did in the past that the Jews are under my protection and I reject any distinction that should be made amongst my people."

However, with the emigration to Israel and tumult from the Israeli-Arab conflict, two pogroms occurred in June 1948. These pogroms targeted two eastern towns, Oujda and Djerrada. Muslim leaders were deeply upset and personally met with victims' families. After these attacks, from 1948-1956, 90% of Moroccan Jews left the country. The poorer went to Israel, while the richer Jews immigrated to Canada and France.

Even though the Moroccan Jews remain relatively scattered, their heritage remains strong.

Piedmontese Charoset

The northern region of Italy, the Piedmont, is surrounded on three sides by the Alps. This region is dotted with nut trees, especially chestnuts. This recipe is rich with chestnuts and other nuts and brings to mind "chestnuts roasting on an open fire."

Makes approximately 2-½ cups

INGREDIENTS

1½ cups cooked & peeled chestnuts

⅔ cup blanched almonds

2 hard boiled egg yolks

zest of 1 orange

juice of 1 orange

⅓ cup sugar

¾ cup sweet red Kosher wine, such as Manischewitz

INSTRUCTIONS

Grind the almonds fine in the food processor, then add the rest of the ingredients and blend to a paste

History:

The main Jewish settlements in Piedmont began in the 15th century and consisted of Jews who escaped persecution in Eastern France. These Jews escaped a few decades after the Spanish persecutions, when in 1492 the Catholic King and Queen of Spain, Ferdinand and Isabella, forced all Jewish and Arab subjects to convert, flee or die on the stake.

Many Jewish families were forced to leave their homes between 1941 and 1943, and lived in the country or in the mountains until the Liberation of the North of Italy in late April 1945. They were concealed by Italian families or by groups of partisans who took the life-threatening risk of hiding Jews.

Despite this, all the Piedmontese Jewish Communities lost a very high number of members in the Nazi-fascist persecutions and deportations. Some of the smaller communities never recovered and closed their Synagogues after the War. This recipe is our attempt to honor their spirit.

Spanish Sephardic Charoset

V, GF

Spanish Sephardic Charoset relies on the local bounty that grows on the Iberian Peninsula. Pears, pistachios, figs and hazelnuts highlight this tapas-style charoset.

Makes approximately 7 cups

INGREDIENTS

2 apples

2 pears

½ cup marcona almonds

½ cup hazelnuts

½ cup walnuts

½ cup pistachios

½ cup chopped dates

½ cup chopped figs

½ cup yellow raisins

¼ tsp ground cloves

½ tsp ground ginger

1 tsp cinnamon

1 tsp lemon zest

½ cup dry red wine

INSTRUCTIONS

Peel, core and finely chop the apples and pears and place in a large bowl

In a food processor, pulse all the nuts

Add the chopped dates, figs and raisins as well as the wine to the food processor

Pulse again briefly in the food processor or mix by hand. Add the mixture to the bowl of chopped apples and pears and stir to combine

Stir in the spices and lemon zest

Yemenite Charoset

Given my extensive travel in the Middle East, I thought that including a charoset from Yemen to highlight the Jewish experience beyond Israel was important and interesting. We hope you will savor the combination of flavors with the dates, raisins, sesame seeds and aromatic spices.

Makes approximately 3 cups

INGREDIENTS

½ cup pomegranate juice

¼ cup sweet red Kosher wine, such as Manischewitz

¾ cup dates, pitted & finely chopped

¼ cup raisins

½ cup almonds, chopped

½ cup walnuts

2 tbsp sesame seeds, toasted (optional)

1 Granny Smith apple, finely chopped (leave peel on)

¼ tsp each ground cinnamon, cloves, cardamom, ginger and cumin

INSTRUCTIONS

In small saucepan, heat pomegranate juice and wine to simmer

Remove from heat and add dates and raisins. Let sit for 5 minutes until they are hydrated and softened then pour into a large bowl

Mix in remaining ingredients. Store in refrigerator. Can be made 2-3 days in advance but add apples at the last minute so they are bright and fresh

PASSOVER

Etrog Marmalade

V, GF

My daughters and I love to cook together. One of the first recipes we ever made together was cranberry jelly for Thanksgiving. We enjoyed the canning process so much that we explored other fruits that we could make into jam or jelly. While celebrating Succot, our Harvest Festival, they asked me if we could eat the etrog, a special citrus fruit used in the Succot holiday. I replied, "Why not?" and developed this recipe for Etrog Marmalade. We make it for Succot then preserve it for Passover.

Originally only grown in the Middle East, etrogs have been planted by Jews all over the world, cultivating the fruit where it can thrive. Our family is obsessed with the etrog. I have an etrog from my childhood, which is now over 40 years old! It may be the oldest etrog in the world.

Makes four 12-oz jars

INGREDIENTS

5 oranges, thinly sliced then quartered

1 etrog, thinly sliced, quartered, seeds removed and tied in cheesecloth

1 lemon, thinly sliced, quartered, seeds removed and tied in cheesecloth

4 cups water

2 cups sugar

1 vanilla bean (optional)

INSTRUCTIONS

Put water and orange, etrog and lemon quarters in a stock pot along with the etrog and lemon seeds that have been tied securely in cheesecloth. The seeds have natural pectin in them which will help thicken your marmalade

If you're adding a vanilla bean, slice it down the middle, scrape out the seeds and put the seeds and the pod in the pot

Bring pot to low boil then simmer for 15 minutes

Add sugar and simmer another 45 minutes or until the marmalade thickens to your liking

Remove cheesecloth bundle and discard

Remove vanilla bean (don't throw away; add to sugar to make delicious vanilla-flavored sugar!)

Pour marmalade into sterilized Mason jars using a funnel if possible to keep the marmalade from getting on the rim of the jar. Or spoon in carefully

Add lid to jar then twist on rim just until the jar turns on its own (about 4 turns). Don't twist tight

Lower jars into a pot of boiling water ensuring the jars aren't directly on the bottom of the pan (rest on other jar lids, a cooling rack or something similar)

Reduce heat and simmer for 15 minutes with cover on the pot

Turn off heat, remove lid and let jars sit in hot water another 5 minutes

Remove jars from pot and set aside at room temperature for 24 hours

Store in a cool, dark place for up to 1 year

Charoset Chicken Salad

This recipe was inspired by Thanksgiving when we have so many great ideas for leftover turkey. We combine the leftover chicken from our Golden Chicken Soup with the Classic Ashkenazi Charoset. The combination of apples, cinnamon and chicken go together perfectly. Enjoy!

INGREDIENTS

Classic Ashkenazi Charoset (see page 15)

cooked chicken

mayonnaise

salt & pepper to taste

INSTRUCTIONS

Mix the charoset with chicken and just enough mayonnaise to hold the chicken salad together

Season with salt and pepper to taste

PASSOVER 33

Emma and Shang at Andy's Bar Mitzvah with Andy's Mom, 1981

We enjoy eating Tzimmes on Passover. It is also served on Rosh Hashanah because it is sweet and symbolizes our hope for a Sweet New Year. This recipe was inspired by my great aunts — Shang and Emma. They were sisters and lived together all of their lives. They were wonderful cooks and always made this delicious Tzimmes for the Jewish holidays. We add a New England flair by including dried cranberries and maple syrup in the dish.

Shang and Emma's Tzimmes

V, GF

Makes approximately 5 cups

INGREDIENTS

2 tbsp extra virgin olive oil

1 red onion, finely chopped

1-¼ cups carrots, peeled & chopped into coins

1-½ cups sweet potatoes, peeled & cubed

juice of 1 orange (or ¼ cup orange juice)

¼ cup maple syrup

½ cup dried cranberries

½ cup dried figs

½ cup Medjool dates

½ tsp pepper

½ tsp cinnamon

pinch of salt

INSTRUCTIONS

Heat olive oil in a hot sauce pan then add red onion

Cook onion on medium — low until soft

Add carrots and sweet potatoes and cook for 1-2 minutes

Add orange juice and maple syrup and cook for 5 minutes on low

Add remaining ingredients and cook until you can pierce the carrots and sweet potatoes with a knife (about 5 more minutes)

PASSOVER

"Lucky" Matzo Balls

What would Chicken Soup be without Matzo Balls?! Some like them light, some make them heavy. In our family we call them sinkers versus floaters. We are a "sinker" family! We like how dense and flavorful they are.

As one of the ways to make Passover more magical for children, I came up with the idea for "Lucky" Matzo Balls. Matzo balls with a surprise inside — a crunchy hidden nugget of gribenes. Everyone enjoys these delectable, flavorful morsels so we thought it would be fun for the kids to find gribenes hidden inside some, but not all, the matzo balls. Voila, the "lucky" matzo ball!

Each year, our kids and our friends' kids get so excited when they sink their spoon into their matzo ball and discover that theirs is one of the "lucky" ones. It turns the ordinary experience of eating matzo ball soup into an extraordinary experience! Fun and laughter all around!

"Lucky" Matzo Balls

Makes approximately 50 small or 25 medium-sized matzo balls

INGREDIENTS

FLOATERS

1½ cups matzo meal

10 eggs

2 tbsp salt

½ cup schmaltz, melted

bowl of water for wetting hands to roll matzo balls

chopped fresh dill (optional — adds nice color and flavor)

SINKERS

1½ cups matzo meal

6 eggs, well beaten

1½ tsp salt

9 tbs schmaltz, melted (½ cup + 1 tbsp)

4 tbsp chicken stock or water

bowl of water for wetting hands to roll matzo balls

chopped fresh dill (optional — adds nice color and flavor)

INSTRUCTIONS

FLOATERS

Separate the eggs into two bowls

Beat the whites until stiff with a hand mixer or stand mixer with whisk attachment

Beat the yolks, schmaltz, salt and chopped dill (if using) until light

Fold the egg whites into the yolks

Gradually add the matzo meal. Stir until smooth

Let rest for 10 minutes at room temperature

Form balls with wet hands and rest on parchment-lined cookie sheet. To make some "Lucky" Matzo Balls, insert a small piece of gribenes (see recipe on page 41) in the center of the matzo ball (we usually put gribenes in a third of our matzo balls)

Carefully drop the balls into boiling salted water or clear soup stock (1 tsp salt to 1 quart water).

Simmer for 20 minutes and serve. Or, drain well and add to our Golden Chicken Soup Stock

SINKERS

Blend the matzo meal with the salt and the schmaltz

Add the well beaten eggs and chopped dill (if using)

Mix thoroughly and add chicken stock or cold water to make a dough firm enough to be shaped into balls. Let rest 15-20 minutes

Form balls with wet hands and rest on parchment-lined cookie sheet. To make some "Lucky" Matzo Balls, insert a small piece of gribenes (see recipe on page 41) in the center of the matzo ball (we usually put gribenes in a third of our matzo balls)

Carefully drop the balls into boiling salted water or clear soup stock (1 tsp salt to 1 quart water)

Simmer for 20 minutes. Drain well and add to our Golden Chicken Soup Stock

NOTES

Freeze your matzo balls. First cook them, separating the "lucky" matzo balls with the gribenes inside from the regular ones if you want to keep track. Freeze on parchment-lined baking sheets. Once frozen, remove from baking sheets and store in freezer in zip-top bags or containers. Be sure to mark which are Sinkers and which are Floaters and of course which have the prized gribenes inside!

Schmaltz and Gribenes

GF

There is nothing that says Jewish cooking more than rendering your own chicken fat and making schmaltz! As a serious chef, I know that homemade schmaltz greatly enhances the taste of both my Chopped Chicken Liver and "Lucky" Matzo Balls.

WHAT ARE GRIBENES?

Gribenes are the crunchy brown bits of rendered chicken skin left in the pan after making schmaltz. When I was a kid, my dad used to love making gribenes and schmaltz. My brothers and I used to enjoy eating the crispy bits of gribenes. It was delicious. No matter how much schmaltz or gribenes I make today, there are never any leftovers.

Makes about ½ cup of schmaltz and ½ cup of gribenes

INGREDIENTS

1 lb chicken fat

1 lb chicken skin (from whole chicken, legs, wings, etc.)

INSTRUCTIONS

In a heavy bottom pan, render the fat and chicken skin on low heat for about 2 hours, stirring occasionally. You can also bake in oven at 250 for about the same amount of time. Just stir it every ½ hour or so

Chicken fat will render down to schmaltz and chicken skin will crisp up and make gribenes which are delicious and a fun surprise in our "Lucky" Matzo Balls

VARIATION

Once the fat and chicken skin has rendered down, you can sauté onions to add more depth of flavor.

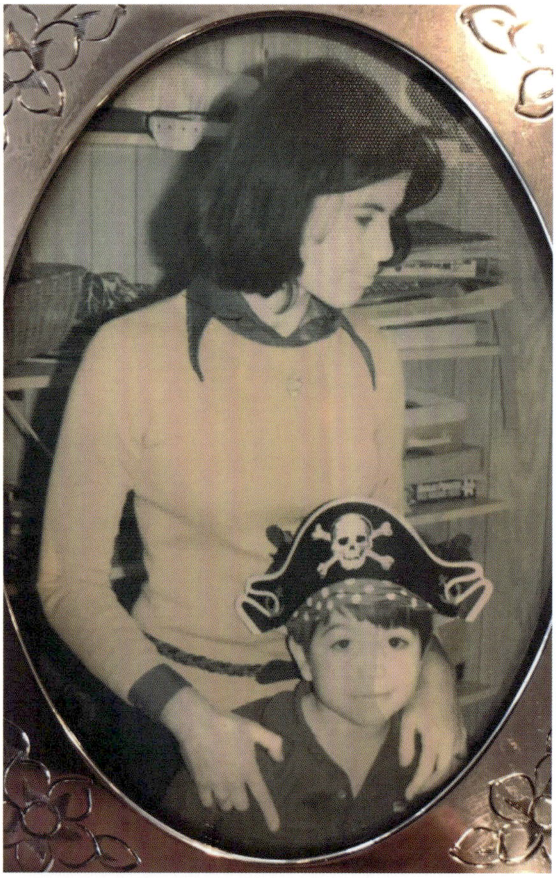

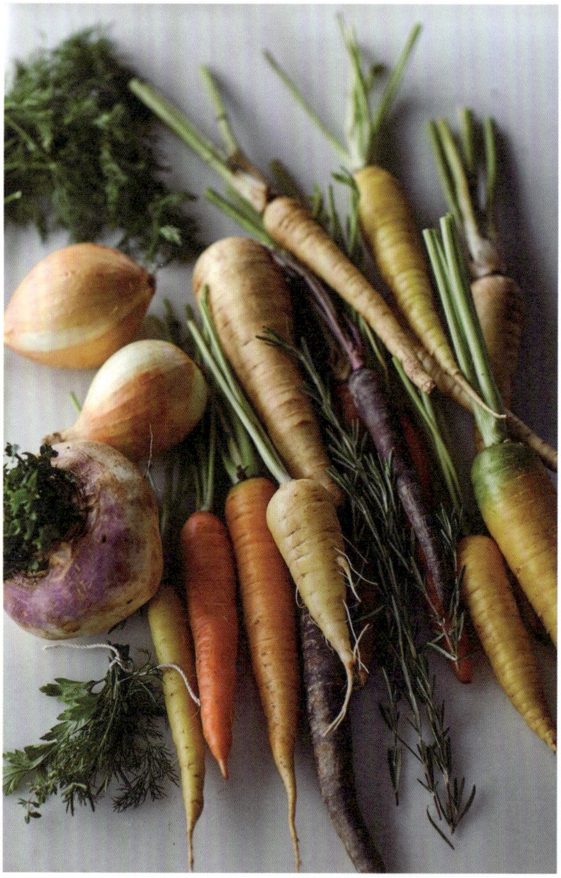

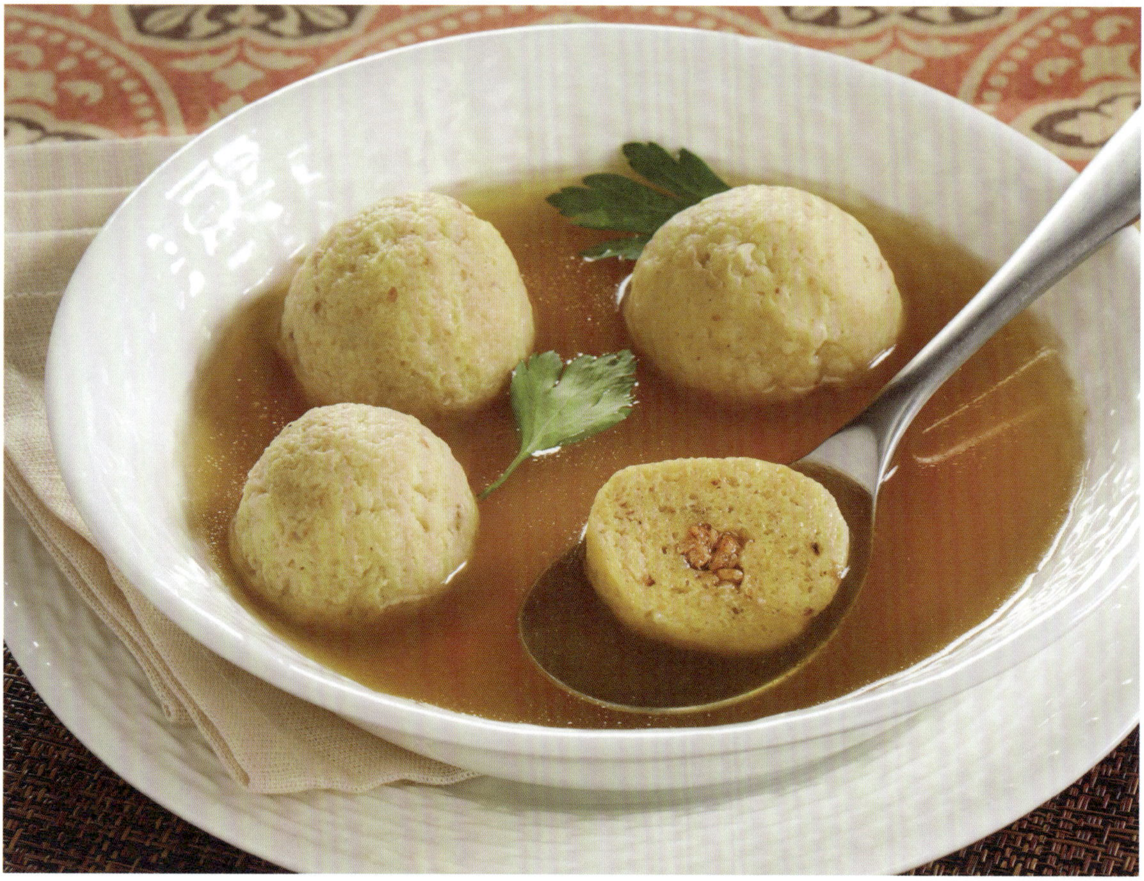

Golden Chicken Soup (Goldena Yoich)

GF

Food equals love in my family. My own ultimate expression of love is to make Chicken Soup with the recipe my mother taught me. I have always made some for my friends and family whenever they are sick. I show up at their door with two big containers of it. A mother's chicken soup is a tangible symbol of the holiness of love. And to this day, I agree. Chicken soup is an essential and edible part of the recipe for love.

Makes about 2 gallons of stock

INGREDIENTS

2 whole chickens (4-5 pounds each)

1 lb chicken drumsticks

1 lb chicken wings

2 lbs chicken necks

6 stalks celery, including the leaves

3 large onions, peeled & rough chopped

6 parsnips, peeled & rough chopped

8 carrots, peeled & rough chopped

2 turnips, peeled & rough chopped

½ celery root or celeriac, peeled & rough chopped

salt & white pepper to taste

herb bundles: tie up 2 bundles of the following herbs with cheesecloth and twine: 3 sprigs fresh parsley, 3 sprigs fresh dill, 3 sprigs of rosemary, 3 sprigs of thyme

INSTRUCTIONS

Place half of the full list of ingredients into a large pot (1 whole chicken, ½ lb drumsticks, ½ lb chicken wings, 1 herb bundle, etc.). Fill pot with enough water to cover ingredients. Bring to a boil then simmer for 3 hours. Remove the scum as it rises to the top of the pot

When broth is done, cool to room temperature and refrigerate overnight

The next day, skim the fat off the top and strain the ingredients from the broth (use the cooked chicken to make Charoset Chicken Salad)

Repeat the stock process and add another batch of all of the ingredients to the strained stock from the previous day. Bring to boil. Simmer for 3 hours. Strain. Cool to room temperature then refrigerate the stock overnight. Skim fat and strain

Serve with our delicious "Lucky" Matzo Balls

NOTES

Recommend making this ahead and freezing in quart containers so you can take them out as you need them.

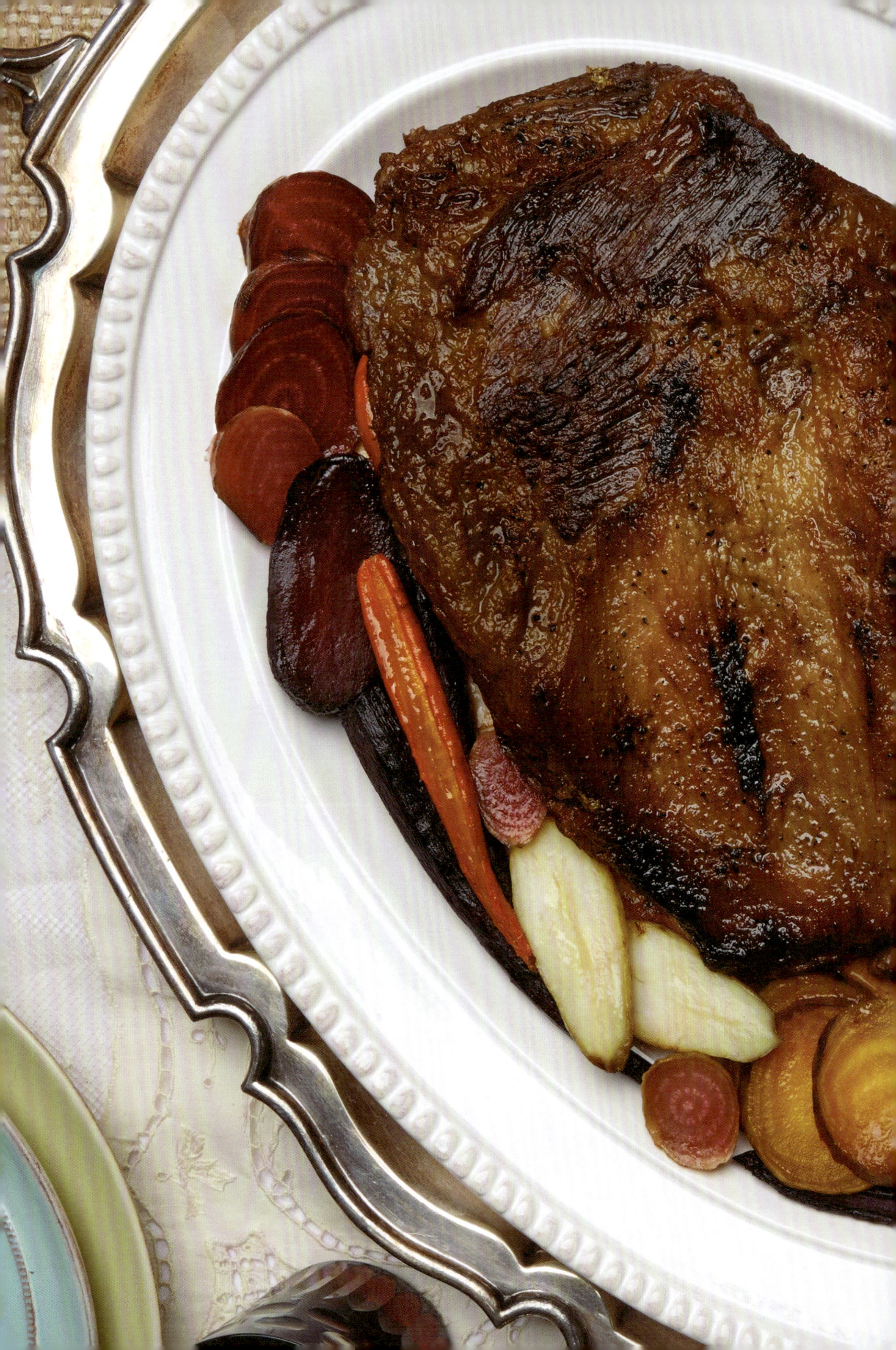

PASSOVER

Grandma Boody's Brisket

Chef Steven Sharad has made this Brisket recipe for our family for over 15 years. Our family and friends have LOVED his recipe. I find it beautiful that he learned this recipe from his grandmother. It is truly made with love.

Serves 8-10

INGREDIENTS

1 beef brisket, 6-8 lbs
2 tbsp vegetable oil
1 pouch Kosher Lipton Onion Soup Mix
2 small cans whole berry cranberry sauce
3 cups water
½ cup red wine (not sweet)
3 large onions, rough chopped
4 carrots, peeled & rough chopped
1 head celery, roughly chopped
salt & pepper to taste

INSTRUCTIONS

Preheat oven to 350°F

Mix the water, onion soup mix and whole berry cranberry sauce together and set aside

Season the brisket with salt and pepper and sear in a large roasting pan in a little bit of vegetable oil until golden brown on both sides. Remove from pan and set aside

Add onions, celery and carrots to the same pan and sauté at a medium-low heat until the vegetables soften (about 10 minutes)

Add the wine and simmer for another 3 to 4 minutes

Nestle the brisket back in the pan with the vegetables and add the onion soup mix, water and cranberry mixture to cover the brisket

Cover roasting pan tightly with aluminum foil and braise brisket in a 350°F oven for about 3 hours. Stick a fork in the brisket, and if it twists easily in the meat, it's done

Remove the meat from the pan and reduce the liquid by a third. Purée the liquid and vegetables all together and check for seasoning. Add additional salt and pepper if needed

Slice the meat against the grain, add the sauce on top and serve with your favorite roasted vegetables

Who needs Katz's Deli when you have leftover brisket?

Freedom Lamb

I was inspired to make this recipe in order to celebrate the Food of Freedom as discussed in the Torah. Pesach is the ritual lamb sacrifice that the Hebrew Slaves were commanded to offer as a public sign that they were about to escape their slavery and become Children of Israel. They placed the blood of the Pesach on their door to be a signal for the angel of death to pass over their home.

While in the wilderness, the Israelites were preparing to enter The Promised Land. They dreamed about the food of The Promised Land — pomegranates, dates, figs and honey. Incorporating all these ingredients into a Passover lamb dish is a nod to the foods of the Israelites' dreams and also makes the connection between the journey of our ancestors and our own journey to freedom, which we celebrate during the Seder meal.

"For the Lord your God is bringing you into a good land, a land with streams and springs and fountains…a land of figs and pomegranates, a land of olive trees and honey; a land where you may eat food without stint, where you will lack nothing… when you have eaten your fill, give thanks to the Lord your God for the good land which he has given to you."
(Deuteronomy 8:7)

Serves 8-10

INGREDIENTS

14 lb lamb shoulder (bone in — ensure there is fat on lamb as that keeps meat moist while braising)

2 tbsp olive oil

2 large onions, peeled & rough chopped

6 carrots, peeled & rough chopped

6 celery spears, roughly chopped

2 cups Manischewitz wine

4 cups beef stock

4 sprigs fresh rosemary + extra for garnish

salt & pepper to taste

1 lb dates, pits removed (approximately 2¼ cups)

1 lb dried figs, halved (approximately 2¼ cups)

1 cup pomegranate molasses

¼ cup honey

1 cup pomegranate seeds

INSTRUCTIONS

Preheat oven to 325°F

Rinse lamb, pat dry and season generously with salt and pepper

Heat large roasting pan on medium heat over two burners and add olive oil. Brown lamb on all sides, remove from pan and set aside

Add onions, carrots and celery to the pan and cook on medium heat until vegetables are slightly softened (about 5 minutes)

Add wine to pan, bring to boil then simmer until reduced by half (about 8 minutes)

Add beef stock and rosemary to pan. Bring to a simmer then remove from heat

Nestle lamb back into the pan, cover roasting pan tightly with aluminum foil and braise in preheated 325°F oven for 3 hours

After the 2-½ hours, add figs and pitted dates to the braising liquid and braise for 30 more minutes covered with the aluminum foil

Take roast out of the oven. Remove lamb from braising liquid and set aside, tented with foil to keep warm

Put roasting pan back over 2 burners on medium heat and reduce braising liquid by half (about 10 minutes)

Stir in pomegranate molasses and honey and simmer for 5 more minutes

Strain braising liquid and serve as gravy. Reserve carrots, figs and dates to serve alongside lamb and discard rest of ingredients

Serve lamb garnished with fresh rosemary sprigs and pomegranate seeds

Matzo Brei

How can we celebrate Passover and not eat Matzo Brei? As a kid, I loved my mom's Matzo Brei for breakfast. The matzo is still crunchy and delicious after soaked in egg (but not too long). You can top Matzo Brei with maple syrup, cinnamon or jam. Our family is in the cinnamon sugar and maple syrup camp. What about yours?

Serves 4

INGREDIENTS

3 sheets matzo

2 large eggs

2 tbsp unsalted butter

INSTRUCTIONS

Lightly beat eggs

Break up matzo into small pieces and soak briefly in the eggs

Heat butter in frying pan on medium-low heat

Spoon matzo mixture into pan to make 4 servings in pancake form

Cook about 3 minutes each side or until egg mixture is cooked through

Serve with maple syrup and cinnamon or jam on top

PASSOVER

Rose Water Almond Cookies

GF

Almonds are very symbolic in Jewish tradition. In Hebrew, "shakad" is the word for almonds. Literally shakad translates to "hasty awakening" or "to watch for." In Israel, the February flowering of the almond trees marks the arrival of spring. The themes of the almond are spring, regeneration, divination and fertility.

Our almond cookies are delicious — crunchy on the outside, chewy on the inside and just a hint of rose water. They are fun and easy to make with the family. Lucy especially loves to be the designated helper when we make these cookies.

Makes about 40 cookies

INGREDIENTS

4 cups blanched almonds plus about 40 almonds, lightly toasted in the oven (or 3 cups almond flour plus 40 almonds)

1 tsp almond extract (optional but adds extra almond flavor)

$\frac{2}{3}$ cup superfine sugar (regular sugar is okay but texture is more tender with the superfine sugar)

3 tbsp rose water

2 eggs, beaten lightly

confectioners sugar to sprinkle on top of cookies

INSTRUCTIONS

Preheat oven to 350°F

Toast 40 almonds in a preheated 350°F oven for about 5-10 minutes (watch so they don't burn). You will top each cookie with an almond before baking

Pulse the 4 cups of blanched almonds in a food processor until the texture resembles coarse flour

Mix the almond flour with the sugar in a bowl

Add the extract, rose water and eggs and mix to a smooth paste with a wooden spoon

Scoop walnut-sized balls onto a parchment-lined cookie sheet and top each with a whole toasted almond

Bake 15-20 minutes or until lightly golden on top and slightly chewy in the middle. Remove immediately from cookie sheet so they don't overbake

Let them cool before dusting with confectioners sugar

NOTES

Food-grade rose water can be purchased on Amazon and in specialty food stores.

Buy almond flour or meal instead of pulsing whole almonds. ¾ cup of almond flour or meal per 1 cup freshly ground almonds.

Freeze cookies fully baked on a flat cookie sheet. Once frozen, remove cookies from cookie sheet and store in freezer in zip-top bags or containers.

PASSOVER

Chocolate Matzo Mousse Cake

As a kid I wondered, why isn't there a really delicious chocolate cake for Passover? My mom came up with this recipe for Kosher Passover (Pesadich) Chocolate Matzo Mousse Cake. It was a winner and is the star dessert of our Passover meal. Sometimes we wonder why we only make it at Passover.

Soaking the matzo in Manischewitz wine gives it a texture like tiramisu. My mom made this recipe with my kids for years. She always let us lick the spatula when she was done mixing the mousse. Delicious!

Serves 8-10

INGREDIENTS

3 cups chilled heavy cream

5 large egg yolks

4 tbsp sugar

1½ tsp vanilla extract

12 oz high quality bittersweet chocolate, chopped plus extra for shaving on top

3 cups sweet red Kosher wine, such as Manischewitz

pinch of salt

8-10 squares of matzo

kosher for Passover non-stick spray

Scan for video

INSTRUCTIONS

PREP PAN

Spray an 8"x8" baking pan with non-stick spray then layer in 2 sheets of parchment paper cut to fit in the pan with enough paper hanging over all 4 sides so you can easily lift the mousse cake out once it has set

MAKE MOUSSE

Heat 1 cup cream in a 1-quart heavy saucepan until hot

Whisk together yolks, sugar and a pinch of salt in a metal bowl until combined well, then add hot cream to egg yolk mixture in a slow stream, whisking constantly so eggs don't curdle

Transfer mixture to saucepan and cook over moderately low heat, stirring constantly, until the custard thickens. Pour custard through a fine strainer into a bowl and stir in vanilla

Melt chocolate in a double boiler or a metal bowl set over a pan of simmering water (or in a glass bowl in a microwave at 50 percent power 3 to 5 minutes), stirring frequently

Whisk custard into chocolate until smooth, then cool in refrigerator for at least 30 minutes, covered with plastic wrap

Beat remaining 2 cups of heavy cream in a bowl with a hand mixer or stand mixer until it just holds stiff peaks

Whisk ¼ of whipped cream into chocolate custard to lighten, then fold in the rest gently but thoroughly

CREATE LAYERS

Use a combination of whole matzo pieces and smaller broken pieces so you can form 5 layers in your 8"x8" pan

Pour Manischewitz in a separate 9"x13" glass baking dish until there's about ½" of wine in the dish

Soak just enough matzo for your first layer for about 2 minutes or until the wine soaks into the matzo. Create your first layer in the bottom of the pan

Add in a thin layer of chocolate mousse over the matzo layer and spread evenly with an offset spatula or the bottom of a spoon. Complete the same process for your next 4 layers

Shave chocolate over the top of the cake and refrigerate for a minimum of 4 hours

To serve, lift the cake out of the pan and cut into squares

Caroline making Chocolate Matzo Mousse Cake

Chocolate Covered Matzo

When I realized how much extra chocolate I had made for the Chocolate Matzo Mousse Cake, I knew I needed a better use for the leftover chocolate aside from just eating it myself. Making Chocolate Covered Matzo is such a fun family activity. My kids LOVE pouring the melted chocolate over the matzo.

INGREDIENTS

bittersweet chocolate chunks or chips

matzo squares

1 jar or container of ready-made caramel

chopped nuts (optional)

INSTRUCTIONS

Melt chocolate in a double boiler or a metal bowl set over a pan of simmering water (or in a glass bowl in a microwave at 50 percent power 3 to 5 minutes), stirring frequently

Lay matzo squares down on parchment paper to keep your counter clean

Pour chocolate generously over matzo squares

Drizzle caramel and sprinkle nuts on top. Enjoy

PASSOVER

Coconut Cheesecake with Candied Lemon Curls

Macaroon and coconut fans will absolutely love this kosher for Passover cheesecake. With a toasted coconut crust, coconut milk in the cheesecake and grated coconut all around the sides of the cake, every bite is a coconut delight. If you're adventurous, we recommend making some Lemon Curls to go on top. The lemon pairs really well with the richness of the cheesecake. It's a dessert that is perfect for Passover, Shabbat or Succot.

PASSOVER

Coconut Cheesecake with Candied Lemon Curls

GF

Serves 8-10 (a small slice is all you need)

INGREDIENTS

CRUST

2 cups sweetened coconut toasted at 350°F for 10 minutes

1 cup melted butter, cooled + extra for greasing the 8" cake pan

1 cup almond flour

1 egg white

CHEESECAKE BATTER

3 packages cream cheese (24 oz total)

1-¼ cups sugar

3 eggs

½ cup full fat coconut milk

1 tsp vanilla extract

1 tbsp lemon juice

1 tsp lemon zest

WHIPPED CREAM TOPPING

1 pint heavy cream

1 tbsp sugar

½ tsp lemon or orange extract

FOR GARNISH

½ to ¾ cup sweetened coconut

¼ cup unsweetened toasted coconut (you can purchase it already toasted)

EXTRA POINTS!

Candied Lemon Curls: If you want to make your cake even more special, add some extra lemon love to the top.

zest of 5-6 lemons (use the side of a lemon zester for best results)

2 cups sugar + 1 extra cup to roll cooked lemon zest in

2 cups water

INSTRUCTIONS

MAKE CANDIED LEMON CURLS (OPTIONAL BONUS!):

Using the notched side of the lemon zester, make 6-8 long thin strands of lemon peel

In a small saucepan, add your water and sugar and simmer on low heat until the sugar is dissolved

Add your lemon strands to the pot and let simmer for 20 minutes

Meanwhile, preheat your oven to 200°F, line a baking sheet with parchment paper and have some metal skewers handy

Remove strands from liquid (save that liquid for cocktails or lemonade!) and roll in bowl of sugar

Wrap each lemon strand around a skewer and lay flat on the baking sheet

Dehydrate lemon curls in the oven for 1 hour or until they are dry and the curl shapes have set

Slide the curls off the skewers and refrigerate in a bowl until you're ready to decorate the cheesecake. You can store extra lemon curls in a container in the refrigerator for a couple of weeks. They make great garnishes for desserts and cocktails

MAKE CRUST

Preheat the oven to 350°F

Spread the sweetened coconut out on a parchment-lined baking sheet and toast for 10 minutes, flipping over a couple times to ensure it doesn't burn

In a medium-sized bowl, combine the toasted coconut, melted butter, almond flour and an egg white. Mix with a wooden spoon until fully combined

Press into an 8" buttered cake pan with a removable bottom making sure to evenly coat the bottom and about ½" up the sides of the pan

Bake for 15 minutes

Remove from oven and let cool

MAKE CHEESECAKE BATTER

Preheat oven to 350°F

Mix the cream cheese and sugar until smooth

Add the eggs one at a time and scrape down the bowl in between as needed to ensure all ingredients are incorporated

Add coconut milk, vanilla, lemon juice and zest and mix just until combined

Pour mixture into cooled crust

Wrap cake pan in tin foil and place in a roasting pan. Pour hot water about a third of the way up the pan. This keeps your cheesecake from cracking

Bake for 1 hour until the cheesecake is set. Insert a toothpick and it should come out clean

Carefully remove pan from oven and remove cheesecake from the roasting pan

Let cool on a rack for about 2 hours

Carefully run a round-edged knife around the outside of the cheesecake and release the cheesecake from the sides of the pan but keep it on the bottom piece

Move your cheesecake to the refrigerator and chill for a minimum of 4 hours

MAKE WHIPPED CREAM TOPPING AND GARNISH THE CHEESECAKE

Whip the cream with the whip attachment of your mixer until soft peaks begin to form

Slowly add the sugar in

Add lemon or orange extract and whip until stiff peaks form

Remove cheesecake from the refrigerator and place on a serving platter (if you want to keep your platter tidy while you decorate, place some pieces of parchment under or very close to the cheesecake. You can remove them when you're finished)

Grab handfuls of the sweetened coconut and press it to the outside of the cake all the way around

Add generous dollops of whipped cream on top and make little peaks and valleys with a spoon

Sprinkle unsweetened toasted coconut all over the top

If you were adventurous and made the Candied Lemon Curls, add a handful on top

Indian-Jewish Sangria

I wanted to highlight the flavors of the Jewish Experience in India. Did you know that Jews have lived in India 2,800 years and were the first foreign religious group to enter the country? It is not surprising that the combination of Indian flavors and Jewish Tradition creates such a delicious and unique recipe.

I adapted my personal Sangria recipe to incorporate an Indian flavor twist! We hope you enjoy our Indian-Jewish Sangria at your Passover Seder or in your Succah during Succot or anytime you would like. It is easy to make and delicious!

INGREDIENTS

3 bottles red wine (we used a dry Israeli Cabernet / Merlot blend)

2 cups (1 pint) sweet red Kosher wine, such as Manischewitz

2 cups mango juice (we used Maaza brand from India)

2 fresh mangoes, peeled & diced

1 large papaya (or 2 small), peeled, seeded and diced

2 lemons sliced into wheels and extra wedges for garnishing the glasses

whole spices for infusing: 1 tsp cloves, 1 tsp cardamom, one 2-inch piece of fresh ginger, 2 cinnamon sticks

ground spices for rimming glasses: mix of 1 tbsp cloves, 1 tbsp cardamom, 1 tbsp ginger, 1 tbsp cinnamon, pinch of cayenne (you can vary these amounts depending on which spices you like best)

Other equipment: cheesecloth and twine

INSTRUCTIONS

Place all ingredients except spices in a large pot

Warm whole spices in a pan on the stove until they become fragrant (2 minutes or so)

Tie spices up in a cheesecloth and submerge in the pot of Sangria

Refrigerate Sangria for a couple of hours or ideally overnight

Before serving, remove cheesecloth and pour Sangria in a pitcher

Moisten rim of glasses with mango juice or water and dip in ground spice blend

Serve over ice with a lemon garnish

NOTES

If you would like your Sangria sweeter, you can make a simple syrup. Pour 1 cup sugar and 1 cup water in a saucepan. Heat until sugar dissolves and add your whole spices. Simmer for 5 minutes then turn off stove. Let sit with cover on for another 10 minutes. Strain, let cool and add simple syrup to the Sangria to your desired sweetness (recommend starting with ½ cup).

PASSOVER

These seder plates are featured in the book *Judaica* by Myra Yellin Goldfarb Outwater (Andy's mother).

PASSOVER

Seder Plate 101

The Seder Plate is the story of Passover on one single plate. The Seder plate is a most efficient and symbolic way to make sure that the major themes of Passover are remembered. Each element on the plate has a specific role in the story of deliverance, and no Passover table is complete without a Seder Plate.

SALT WATER

Salt water represents the tears and emotion of slavery. The double dipping of vegetables signifies the crossing of two bodies of water, Sea of Reeds and Jordan River, to freedom and The Promised Land.

BEITZAH (ROASTED EGG)

The roasted egg represents life. It is roasted to signify the end of "old" life and a move to the future and because fire is both cleansing and a transformation.

KARPAS (VEGETABLE)

The fresh herb reminds us of spring, hope and renewal. It can be any fresh green herb, typically parsley but dill or any other fresh herb will do.

MAROR (BITTER HERBS)

Maror is a bitter tasting herb. Bitter Herbs recall the bitterness of the slavery of the Hebrew Slaves in Egypt and remind us of bitterness and suffering, in our own lives and in the lives of others around the world.

Scan for video

ZEROAH (ROASTED SHANK BONE)

The lamb shank bone is a symbol of the lamb (Pesach in Hebrew) which was sacrificed the night before the Children of Israel were led out of Egypt. Placing the lamb's blood over the entrance of their home was a signal to God to have the Angel of Death pass over the Children of Israel's homes and spare the life of their first born.

Without this sacrifice, each first born child would have been sacrificed. Those in Egypt had two choices: to sacrifice their own child and give up their future or to sacrifice the lamb and make the first step to escape Slavery in Egypt and begin the journey of freedom to The Promised Land.

CHAROSET (MORTAR)

Charoset is a sweet paste made of fruits and nuts. It represents mortar and slavery, recalling the mud that Hebrew slaves used to secure the bricks for Pharaoh's monuments. Charoset is sweet because slavery can be familiar, and we can endure it for a certain period of time.

CHARAZET (MORE BITTER HERBS)

See above.

PASSOVER

Passover Discussion Questions

We hope that these questions will stimulate a meaningful discussion at your Seder.

1. **What are you a slave to today? Why?**

    Passover is the story of the Children of Israel seeking freedom, wandering in the Wilderness and reaching freedom in the Promised Land.

    We are all slaves to something today. Not physical slaves but slaves in our own mind.

    Kids: What do you think about the most? You may be a slave to electronics, video games or your favorite television show.

    Adults: Are we slaves to our past? Or maybe slaves to worry, work, financial pressure or scheduling?

2. **What represents your Promised Land? What is freedom to you?**

    During Passover, we celebrate the story of the Children of Israel seeking freedom in the Promised Land. But what does being free really mean to each of us?

    Kids: You may feel really free during summer vacation, summer camp, sleepovers, walking your dog or attending a sporting event. When do you feel most free?

    Adults: What does freedom look like to you? When are you truly free? On vacation? Engaging in a special family activity? Cooking dinner with friends? Going for a long hike? Is freedom just having unscheduled time? Do you have a favorite activity when you feel most free in your mind and spirit?

3. What are your basics in your life? What are your extras?

   Matzo is a very simple food. The word "matzo" in Hebrew means to "drain out." Food at its most basic. Only flour and water, oil and salt. Matzo kept the Children of Israel alive while they were wandering in the wilderness. Eating matzo makes us think about the basics in life. What do you really need to live your life?

   Kids & Adults: What do you really need in your life? What do you really need to live your life?

   Kids & Adults: What are the basics in your life? What are your extras?

4. If you had to leave home in the middle of the night, what would you bring with you?

   When the Children of Israel left Egypt, they had to leave in the middle of the night without much time to prepare. And they couldn't take many possessions with them on their journey. There were difficult choices about what to bring with them from their homes.

   If you had to escape in the middle of the night, what would you bring? (These can be physical or emotional keepsakes).

   Kids & Adults: What would you take from your house in the middle of the night if you had to leave?

PASSOVER

Passover
Discussion Questions Continued

5. **Other than Elijah, who would you like to sit in Elijah's chair at your Seder?**

    Elijah is the prophet who never died. He is viewed as eternally returning to help the poor and assist those in need. When we invite Elijah to join our Seder, we receive a special blessing because we remember his good deeds.

    The special cup for Elijah, and in some families a chair for Elijah, is a reminder to invite the spirit of generosity and goodness to join us at the Seder.

    In some families, the children go to the door and open it for Elijah to enter.

    Kids: Who is missing from our table this evening? Who do we need to invite in?

    Kids & Adults: What special person would you most like to share tonight's festive meal? This person can be alive today, or not. It might be a friend, relative or someone that you would like to meet. Please share who this person is and why you would like to share tonight's Seder with them.

    Adults: Whom do we need to help us complete our journey from "slavery" to "freedom?" Who helps each of us become complete? Who or what do we need to lead us on our journey to freedom?

6. **The Afikoman is created by breaking an ordinary piece of matzo. What is something ordinary that has become extraordinary for you?**

    We think a lot about transformation from the ordinary to the extraordinary during our Seder.

    A good example is the Afikoman. We ate matzo at the start of our journey out of slavery, but during the Passover Seder, we transform this simple humble food. We take one ordinary piece of matzo and by breaking it in half, it becomes an extraordinary piece of matzo: the Afikoman.

    One example of something ordinary to extraordinary in my life is my family's antique brass hand washer. I received it as a gift from my grandmother, Helen Fish Goldfarb. Her father, my great grandfather Max Fish received it from his father (my children's great great grandfather Moshe Fish). It is from the late 1800s in Dynow Poland and has been used for Passover in our family for over 100 years. Perhaps your family has an artifact or heirloom that has been handed down over the generations, layered with the history of your family, and so has become "extraordinary."

    What is something ordinary in your life that you have transformed into something extraordinary?

    Kids: Is there something special you have transformed in your life because you love it so much? Maybe a special blanket or doll? Or something you received from a special relative, or is it something you made? Something you have transformed by how much you love it and need it?

    Adults: How do you know that it has become extraordinary? Do others or just yourself know this transformation? Do you have a "public" Afikoman and a "private" Afikoman?

7. **Dayenu means "enough." It is an expression of gratitude. When was a time in your life that you truly experienced Dayenu? And expressed gratitude?**

    In Hebrew, Dayenu means "enough for us." We both sing it and say it many times during the Seder. Dayenu can be an opportunity to recognize your best efforts. Or, that you received a bountiful offering from someone else.

    On one level, Dayenu speaks about giving thanks to God for delivering the Children of Israel into the Promised Land. On another level, it is a message about setting limits on our expectations. Dayenu is about learning to be satisfied and grateful with what we have received.

    Kids: Can you think of a time when you received something in your life that you are grateful for?

    Adults: Was there a time in your life that you didn't experience Dayenu, when you didn't appreciate that you had received "enough," but should have?

8. **Miriam led the Children of Israel in celebration after crossing the Sea of Reeds. What does it mean to be someone who leads others in rejoicing? When have you ever danced for pure joy to celebrate? How did it feel? What was the response of the group to your dance?**

    In Exodus after the Children of Israel escaped from the Egyptians through the parted Sea of Reeds and arrived safely on dry ground, Miriam took out her timbrel and led the Israelite women in dance and song to celebrate.

    When I was in Israel for my daughter's Bat Mitzvah at a restaurant on the Lake in Tiberias, there was another family's Bar Mitzvah celebration, and I impulsively crashed the party and led my family in dancing the Hava Nagilah with the rest of the party. It was so much fun!

Kids: When have you started a really fun celebration dance with your friends? What was the occasion? How did they react?

Adults: When have you really let loose for pure celebratory dance? I always think of the fun of dancing the Hava Nagilah and raising the Hora Chair at weddings and Bar/Bat Mitzvahs.

9. **The Sea of Reeds was the final obstacle for the Children of Israel to overcome in escaping Slavery. What is your personal Sea of Reeds (final) obstacle in your journey from Slavery to achieve Freedom?**

When the Children of Israel escaped from slavery in Egypt, they faced one final obstacle before reaching freedom. They had to cross the Sea of Reeds. In Exodus 14:15 God tells Moses that the Children of Israel are to go forward. They are being asked to take the first step. And what is the first step? To walk towards un-parted waters. It is an act of faith that precedes God's act of liberation. And so it is with our lives. The first step is ours. Then Moses is instructed to raise his staff and the waters parted, allowing the Children of Israel to leave the past, pass the present and look to the future to truly cross over — Ivrit is Hebrew meaning to "cross over."

Kids: Have you ever tried to do something new and had an obstacle? How did you overcome it?

Adults: What has been your final obstacle as you have tried to escape from slavery, or break a bad habit or start a new relationship? How did you overcome the obstacle? Did you ever proceed without knowing the solution in advance?

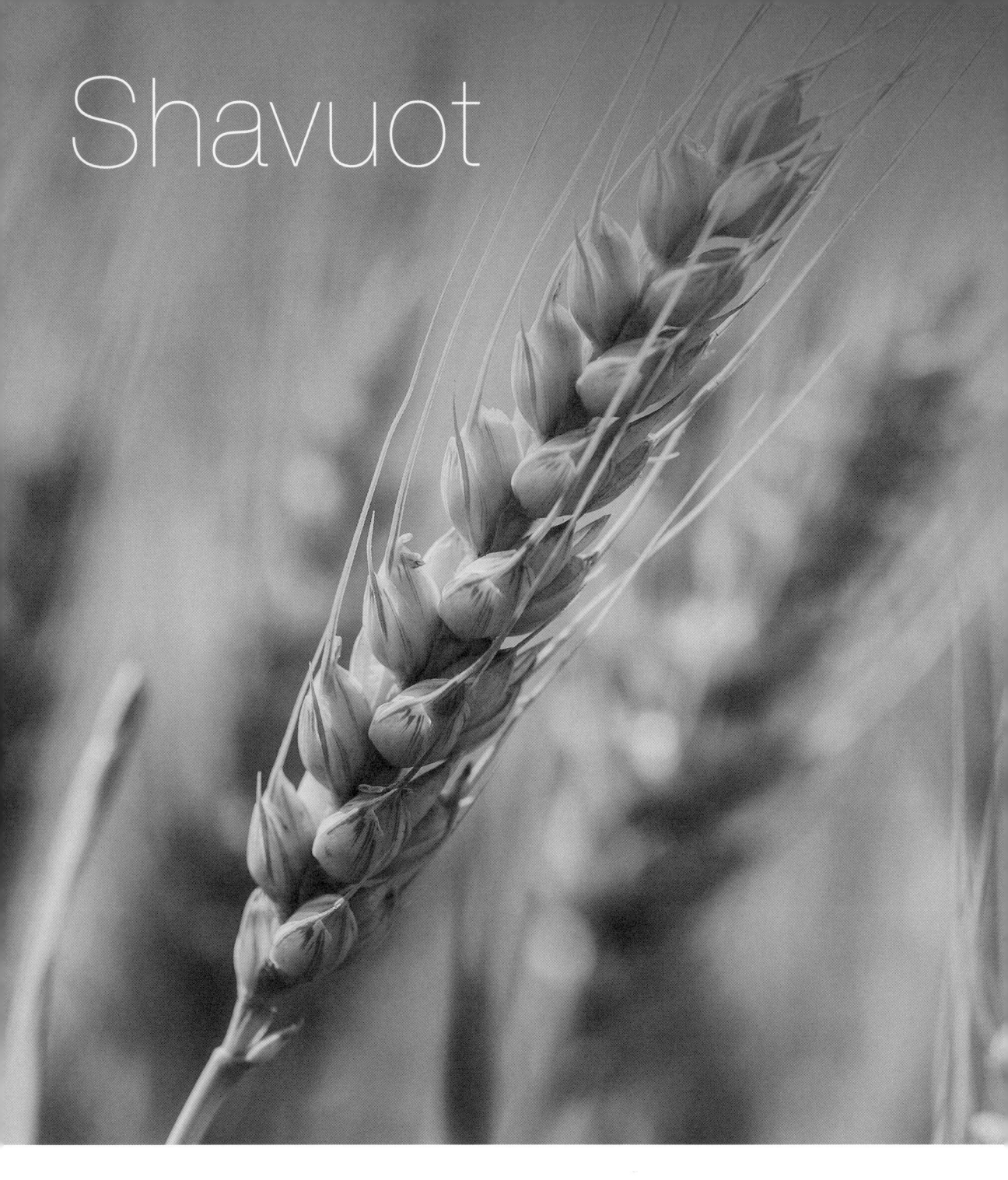

Shavuot

Shavuot, along with Passover and Succot, is part of the Shalosh Regalim, the three major pilgrimages in the Jewish calendar, when people come together in Jerusalem and offer their agricultural gatherings. For Shavuot, Ancient Israelites brought their first gathering of fruits as an offering to God. Shavuot marks the time of year in which the wheat harvest starts and barley harvest ends as well as the time that the Torah was passed onto the Israelites on Mount Sinai. With origins that tie to ancient mid-summer harvest celebrations from the Canaanites, "Sheva" in Hebrew means seven, and similar sounding "Shavuot" is the plural of Sheva and signifies the importance of the number seven in Judaism. There were seven days of creation in Genesis. Shavuot marks the end of the seven weeks of seven days after Passover and on the 50th day, the festivities begin.

Shavuot

Shavuot, the Festival of Weeks, is one of the three pilgrimage festivals in the Torah, along with Passover in the spring and Succot in the fall. While Succot and Passover are each a week long, Shavuot is only one day (two days for many Jews outside of Israel), and at first glance it lacks the color and zest of the previous two holidays. But first impressions can be deceiving.

Shavuot is unique among the Bible's holidays in that it does not have a fixed date in the Hebrew calendar, unlike Rosh Hashanah, Yom Kippur, Passover and Succot. Shavuot comes 50 days after Passover, and the name the "festival of weeks" highlights the connection between these two holidays. It is also called the holiday "of the first fruits" and "of the harvest." Shavuot's content in the Torah is agricultural, referring to the wheat which hopefully has grown well and is ripe at this time. Colorful ceremonies of "first fruit offerings" are still very common today in Israel at *kibbutzim* and *moshavim* (communal and shared farms), even if they are not religious.

The Torah gives clear historical, as well as agricultural, reasons for Passover (the exodus from Egypt) and Succot (the little huts the Children of Israel slept in during the wandering in the desert). Shavuot in the Torah has no historical function. The tradition that the Torah was given to Moses and the Jews at Mount Sinai on Shavuot comes later, about 2000 years ago, in the Rabbinic tradition (the Talmud). It took some clever interpretation; the Torah does not specify the date of the revelation at Sinai either. Assigning it to Shavuot adds an important spiritual dimension to the holiday.

Over the centuries a number of traditions have developed around Shavuot. Many people decorate their homes and synagogues with greens, and the giving of the Torah is recalled in all-night learning sessions. Jerusalem, Tel Aviv and many communities in Israel are busy all night, with people wandering for study from one place to the next. And there's an old and popular custom for people to eat dairy foods on the holiday, recalling the verse in Song of Songs 4:11 *"milk and honey are under your tongue."* Others say the Torah nurtures the Jewish people the way a mother's milk nurtures the new-born. And the Book of Ruth recounts a touching story of kindness and inclusion, how a Moabite woman became the great-grandmother of King David, is read on Shavuot. Shavuot is a lovely holiday that can be celebrated both with community in the synagogue and with family or friends in the home.

Andy's Aunt and Uncle
Dr. Ada Goldfarb and
Rabbi Daniel Goldfarb

Classic Cheese Blintzes

Cheese Blintzes are a great dairy option for Shavuot and are connected to milk and honey, two ingredients that describe and celebrate the land of Israel: Eretz Zavat Chalav U'dvash (Land of Milk and Honey).

God will "rescue [the Hebrews] from the Egyptians and bring them…to a land flowing with milk and honey." (Exodus 3:8)

If there is one perfect breakfast, brunch, lunch, dinner or snack in the repertoire of Jewish cuisine, we vote for the Cheese Blintz. Tidy packages of golden pancakes stuffed with a sweet mild cheese and pan-fried to perfection. Hot, warm or cold, it's a hard dish to resist. My great Aunts, Shang and Emma, used to make me these delicious blintzes as a kid.

They are classics on the Hanukkah holiday table too (referencing the Hanukkah holiday's traditional spotlight on foods with cheese, sweetness and oil). But we depend on this recipe for our Yom Kippur Break Fast as well as for Bar/Bat Mitzvah Kiddush luncheon.

Makes 8-10 blintzes

INGREDIENTS

BATTER

- 3 large eggs
- 2 egg yolks
- ½ cup milk
- 1 tbsp sugar
- pinch of salt
- ¾ cup canola oil
- 1 cup flour
- ¼-½ cup water (as needed)
- non-stick cooking spray for pan
- butter for browning (have about 6 tbsp on hand)

FILLING

- 12 oz cream cheese
- 2 cups ricotta
- zest of 1 lemon
- 1 tbsp lemon juice
- 1 tsp vanilla
- ½ cup sugar
- pinch of salt

FOR SERVING

- sour cream
- apple sauce

INSTRUCTIONS

MAKE CREPE BATTER

Whisk together all ingredients except flour

Sift in flour gradually and blend well

Add water as needed to thin the batter for easy pouring

Refrigerate batter for 30 minutes

MAKE CREPES

Heat a non-stick 8" frying pan over medium heat

Coat pan with non-stick cooking spray

Pour approximately ¼ cup batter into the pan and swirl the batter around quickly to form a thin crepe

Cook crepes 1 at a time, 1 side only. This will take about 45 seconds

Slide crepe out of the pan and repeat until you use all the batter

MAKE FILLING

Combine filling ingredients until smooth in a food processor, blender or by hand

It not making the blintzes right away, refrigerate the filling

ADD FILLING & COOK BLINTZES

For assembly, portion ¼-½ cup of filling in the middle of the blintz

Fold top down over filling, fold in the two sides, then fold over to close in the filling

Heat 1 tbsp butter in the pan on medium heat. Add 2 blintzes to the pan at a time

Flip after 1-2 minutes until lightly browned

Serve immediately with your choice of sour cream, apple sauce, berries and confectioners sugar

NOTES

Blintzes freeze well. Just don't cook them. Freeze them stuffed and rolled. Place flat on a cookie sheet sprayed with non-stick cooking spray. Once frozen, remove and place in a zip-top bag. When you want to prepare them, defrost completely and brown them in a pan with butter.

Succot

APPETIZERS
Kafta (Lebanese Lamb Kebabs)
Ground Beef and Thyme Stuffed Baby Artichokes
Sephardic Lamb Meatballs with
Kosher Cashew Dipping Sauce
Roasted Garlic Hummus
Baba Ganoush
Butternut Squash Soup
Parsnip and Apple Soup
Fattoush Salad
Tabbouleh

ENTREES
Shakshuka
Butternut Squash Lasagna
Quinoa and Vegetable Stuffed Acorn Squash
Moroccan Inspired Vegan Stuffed Artichokes
Spaghetti Squash with Basil and Kale Pesto

Succot is the Festival of Booths. Celebrated in the fall four days after Yom Kippur, it is a 7-day celebration of the harvest and is a time for communal celebration following the intensity of the High Holy Days. We go all out for our Succot, setting up a beautiful succah (booth) in the backyard and inviting friends and family over to enjoy a seasonal feast and to give thanks for the bounty of life. Dwelling in a succah is also a sign of trust — even as the winter approaches, we trust that God will provide for us throughout the cold and dark months ahead.

We use as many fall harvest New England ingredients as possible at our Succot. You'll find apples, pears and squash appear in many of our recipes. We also serve many warm dishes to ward off the chill in the air — meatballs, lasagna, lamb skewers and seasonal soups like Butternut Squash, Parsnip and Apple.

DESSERTS
Apple Honey Cake
Apple Rose Pastries
Vanilla and Anise Poached Pears

BEVERAGE
Apple Cider Hot Toddy

V = Vegan
GF = Gluten Free

Kafta (Lebanese Lamb Kebabs)

GF

Whenever we make Lebanese Kafta for guests, the skewers disappear within minutes! Our secret to keeping them nice and moist is to add a little apple sauce to the lamb mixture. Serve with our Tabbouleh, Fattoush or Israeli Salad, Tahini Sauce and Pita. This is a perfect dish for your Succot celebration or Shabbat dinner.

Makes about 12-14 kebabs depending on size of patty

INGREDIENTS

1-½ lbs ground lamb

½ cup apple sauce

1 bunch scallions, finely chopped

½ cup fresh mint, chopped

2 tbsp Lebanese 7-Spice* (or you can use equal parts cumin & smoked paprika)

juice and zest of 1 lemon

½ red onion, finely chopped

1 tbsp olive oil

salt & pepper to taste

*Lebanese 7-Spice: There are variations on what the 7 spices are but the blend we used contains: allspice, pepper, cinnamon, cloves, nutmeg, fenugreek and ginger

INSTRUCTIONS

Mix all ingredients in a large bowl and form into rectangular patties, slightly flattened to ensure they cook through. Cover with plastic wrap and refrigerate for a minimum of 30 minutes (you can make several hours ahead)

When ready to grill or broil, remove from refrigerator, skewer each patty and brush each with a little olive oil so it doesn't stick to the grill or pan

Grill or broil 4 minutes each side or until meat is cooked to your liking

NOTES

If you use wooden skewers, avoid burning them while cooking by soaking them for a few hours in water and/or cover the part of the grill or broiler where the skewers will rest with tin foil.

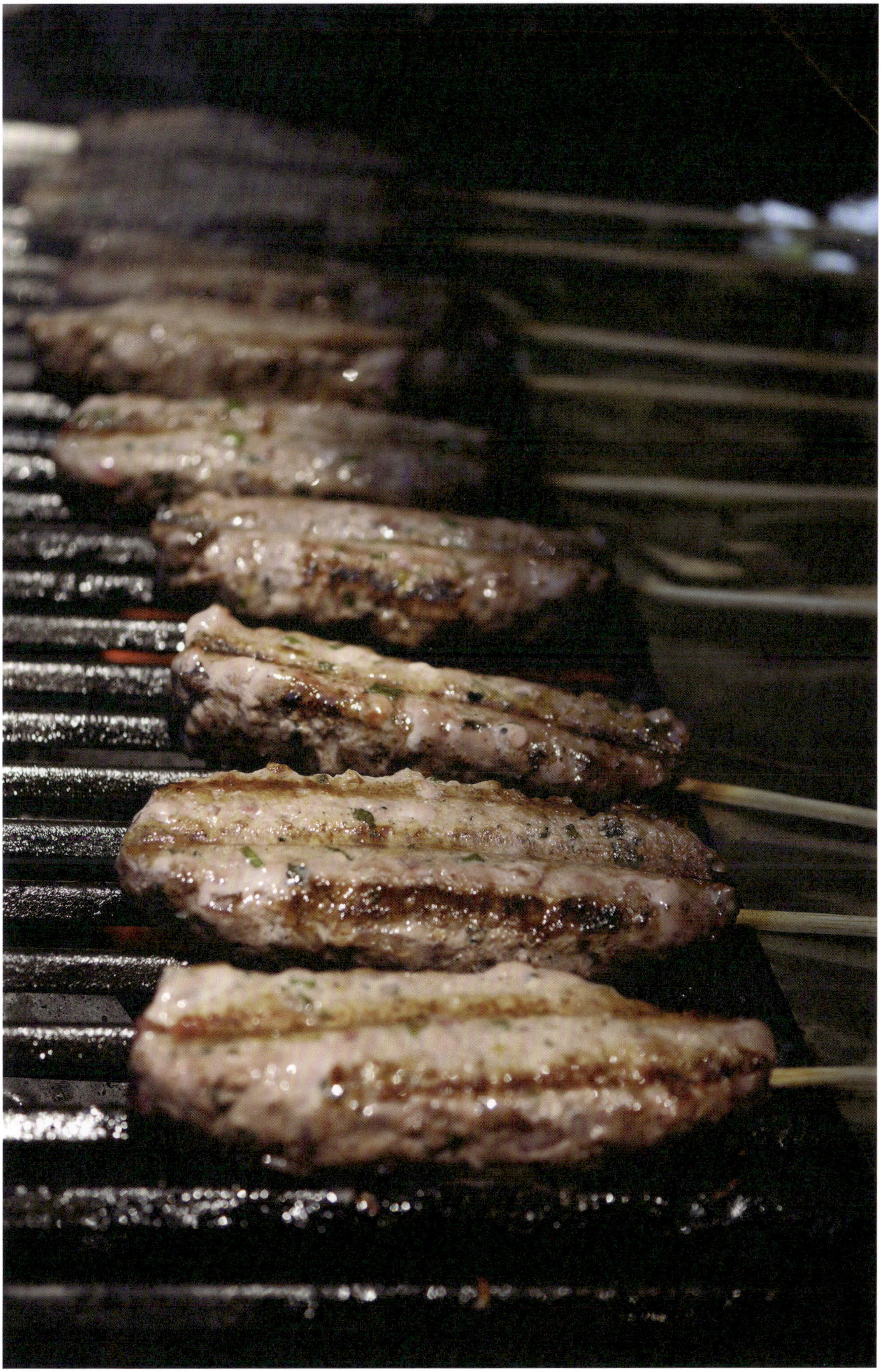

Ground Beef and Thyme Stuffed Baby Artichokes

GF

The hearty meat stuffing of this dish makes for a satisfying appetizer. You can create the stuffing a couple days ahead and only worry about prepping and stuffing the artichokes on the day you serve them. Lots of flavor and quite filling. Perfect for a warm snack in your succah or as part of your Shabbat meal!

Makes 12 appetizers

INGREDIENTS

FOR ROASTED ARTICHOKES

6 baby artichokes

1 lemon, quartered

1 tsp olive oil

pinch of salt

FOR GROUND BEEF STUFFING

¼ lb ground beef

½ cup fresh chopped tomato

2 tbsp olive oil

2 tbsp scallions, finely chopped

juice of ½ lemon

1 tbsp pine nuts

1 small clove garlic, minced

2 tsp fresh thyme, roughly chopped + extra for garnish

2 tsp fresh ginger, minced

1 tsp cumin

pinch of cayenne pepper

salt & pepper to taste

INSTRUCTIONS

FOR ROASTED ARTICHOKES

Preheat oven to 400°F

Fill a bowl with water and squeeze the juice of the lemon quarters into the bowl. Add the lemons to the bowl

Prep baby artichokes: cut off ½" from the top and a little off the bottom, remove tough outer layers and submerge in lemon water while you prep the rest of your artichokes (recommend wearing gloves when removing leaves — they are sharp and may give you splinters)

Remove artichokes from lemon water and pat dry with a paper towel

Toss artichokes with olive oil and salt and roast cut side down for 15-20 minutes (you want them to be slightly browned on the cut side) then flip and roast on the other side for 5 minutes. While artichokes are roasting, make your Ground Beef Stuffing

FOR GROUND BEEF STUFFING

Heat skillet on medium heat. Add oil, scallions and ginger and sauté until soft (about 1-2 minutes)

Add cumin, cayenne and fresh thyme and cook for 1 minute, stirring frequently

Add beef and cook through (about 3 minutes) breaking up large pieces of meat with the back of a wooden spoon

Add tomatoes and cook for 1-2 minutes until tomato breaks down and binds with the meat mixture

Add salt and pepper to taste. Set aside

ASSEMBLY

Place artichoke halves cut side up on a plate and spoon about a tablespoon of ground beef stuffing on each half

Garnish with fresh thyme or parsley

SUCCOT

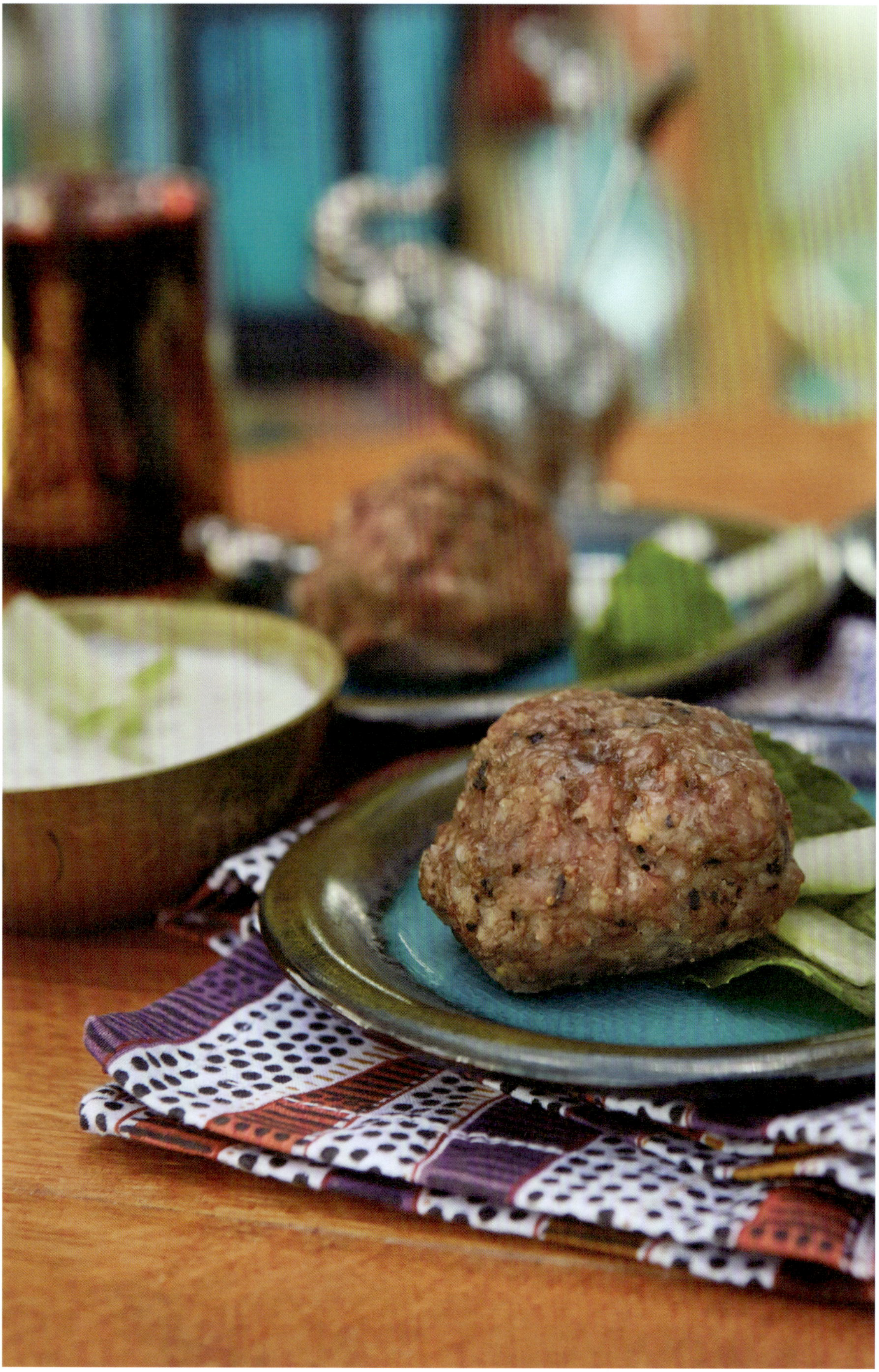

Sephardic Lamb Meatballs with Kosher Cashew Dipping Sauce

GF

This recipe reminds us of Sephardic Jews celebrating in their Moroccan style succah. The ground pine nuts add a great texture to the meatballs and the fresh mint and apple sauce gives the meatballs a bright, slightly sweet flavor. Serve appetizer style and if you'd like a dipping sauce, try our delicious Kosher Cashew Dipping Sauce.

Makes 25-30 meatballs depending on size

INGREDIENTS

FOR MEATBALLS

- 2 lbs ground lamb
- ½ red onion, roughly chopped
- 2 tbsp pine nuts
- 2 cloves garlic
- 1 cup fresh mint
- ¼ cup apple sauce (for moisture and a little sweetness)
- 1 tbsp cumin
- 1 tbsp salt
- 1 tsp pepper
- 1 egg, lightly beaten

FOR KOSHER CASHEW DIPPING SAUCE

- ¼ cup olive oil
- ½ cup water
- 1 cup raw, unsalted cashews
- juice of 1 lemon
- 1 clove garlic
- 1 tsp salt
- pepper to taste
- 1 tbsp chopped fresh herbs (dill, oregano or fennel fronds — the wispy pieces that look like fennel attached to the fennel bulb)

INSTRUCTIONS

FOR MEATBALLS

Preheat oven to 350°F

Line a baking sheet with parchment paper

In a food processor, pulse pine nuts, onion, garlic and mint

In a large bowl, combine pulsed ingredients with remaining ingredients

Form meatballs of desired size

Take a small piece of the meatball mixture and cook on stovetop to ensure it is seasoned to your taste. Adjust if needed

Place meatballs on baking sheet and bake for 20-25 minutes (to test doneness with a meat thermometer, meatballs should be 160°F)

Serve appetizer style with toothpicks as is or with our Kosher Cashew Dipping Sauce

FOR KOSHER CASHEW DIPPING SAUCE

Put cashews in a bowl, cover with water and soak overnight or a minimum of 3 hours (this makes the cashews easier to blend and creamier)

Strain cashews and put in food processor with all ingredients except olive oil

As food processor is running, slowly drizzle in olive oil until dip is nice and creamy

Serve at room temperature or chill. This dip is perfect with the Lamb Meatballs and also a great dip for crudité

NOTES

You can make the meatballs ahead and freeze them in a single layer on a baking sheet and then place them in a zip-top bag and place back.

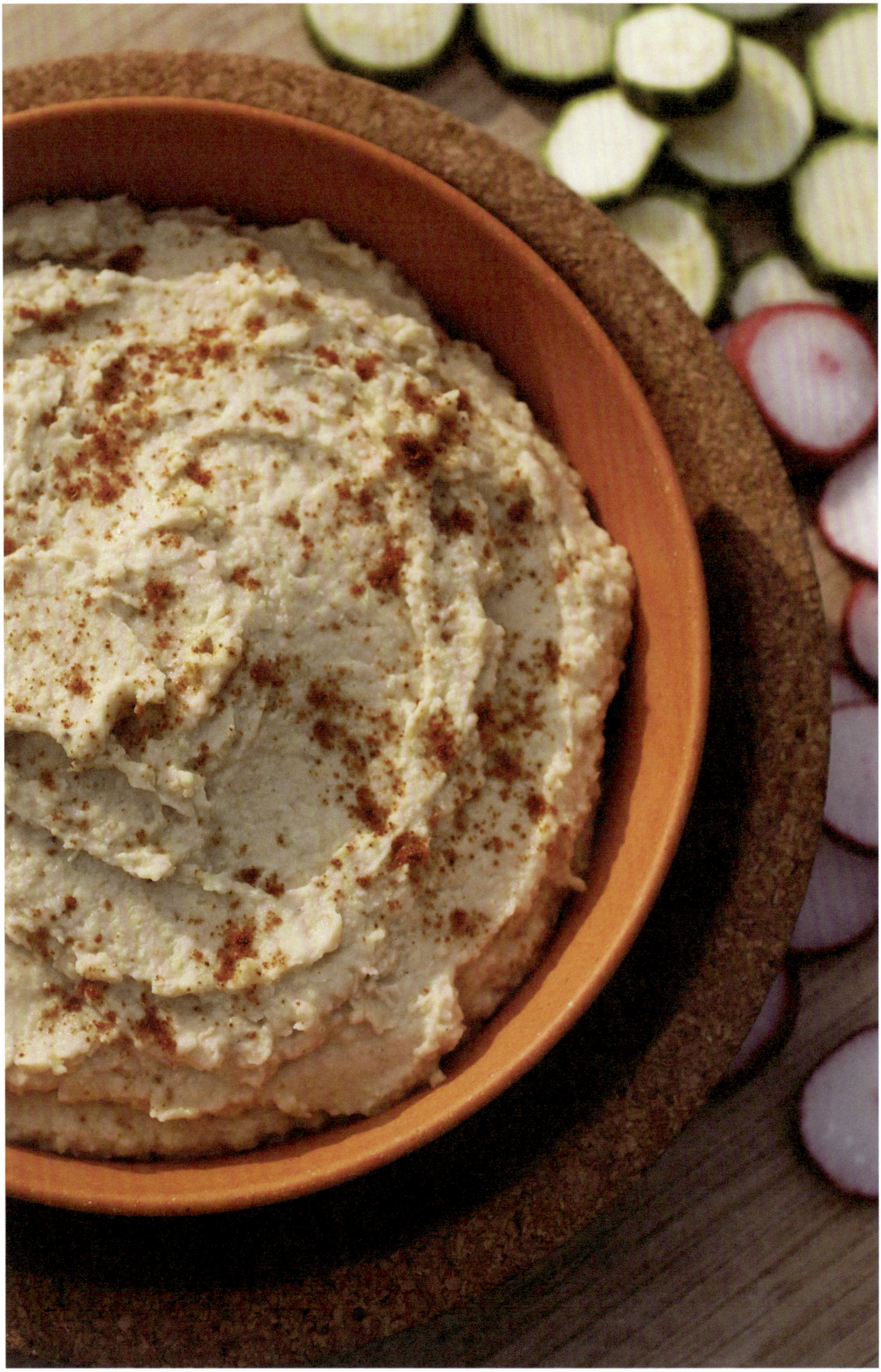

Roasted Garlic Hummus

V, GF

The key to the perfect hummus is to soak dried chickpeas overnight instead of using canned chickpeas. The chickpeas are a little more firm and a lot more flavorful. We like to serve our hummus with sliced wheels of our favorite seasonal veggies or with crackers.

Serves 6-8

INGREDIENTS

2 cups chickpeas

pinch of baking soda

1 head of roasted garlic (see Instructions)

¼ cup fresh lemon juice

⅓ cup tahini

2 tbsp olive oil

⅛ tsp asafetida powder (optional but adds nice flavor)

salt & pepper to taste

INSTRUCTIONS

ROAST GARLIC

Preheat oven to 375°F

Cut off the short end of a whole head of garlic so you can squeeze the cloves out easily after it's roasted

Wrap the whole head of garlic in tin foil and roast on a cookie sheet for 45 minutes - 1 hour (until the cloves soften enough to spread like butter)

PREPARE CHICKPEAS & MAKE HUMMUS

Cover chickpeas with water and soak overnight with a pinch of baking soda (makes chickpeas softer)

Drain and rinse thoroughly

Bring a large pot of water to a boil and cook chickpeas until tender, about 2 hours

Put chickpeas in a food processor

Squeeze 3-4 roasted garlic cloves into the food processor

Add lemon juice, tahini, olive oil, asafetida powder, salt and pepper and purée to a smooth consistency. Add a little more olive oil if necessary

Baba Ganoush

V, GF

—

Lebanese Baba Ganoush is delicious nestled in on a plate with meat and chicken or as a dip or condiment. If you have access to a grill or fire pit, grilling the eggplant is the way to go. The smoky flavor of the eggplant really makes for a show-stopping Baba Ganoush. If not, roasting in the oven is fine as well. Either way, rest assured it'll quickly disappear from your table. This dish would be a delicious part of your Succot meal or Shabbat luncheon. Super healthy and easy to make in advance.

Makes about 4 cups

INGREDIENTS

2 large eggplants

2 garlic cloves, finely minced

¼ cup tahini

juice of 1 lemon

2 tbsp olive oil + extra for drizzling over the finished dish

1 tsp of Lebanese 7-Spice* or equal parts cumin & smoked paprika

salt to taste

1 tbsp of pine nuts, toasted (optional garnish)

*Lebanese 7-Spice: There are variations on what the 7 spices are but the blend we used contains: allspice, pepper, cinnamon, cloves, nutmeg, fenugreek and ginger

INSTRUCTIONS

Grill the eggplants whole on medium heat, rotating occasionally, until they are soft (about 45 minutes). Alternatively, roast them in the oven. Rub a little olive oil on the eggplants and roast them in a 425°F oven on a unlined baking sheet for 40-50 minutes (flip over after 20 minutes) until soft. Split cooked eggplants and scoop out the flesh. Discard exterior

Put eggplant flesh in bowl and add garlic, lemon juice, tahini, olive oil and salt. Pulse in a food processor until smooth. Add a little more lemon juice or water to thin out if necessary

SERVING SUGGESTION

Pour a small pool of olive oil in the middle and top with toasted pine nuts

You can add more or less tahini and lemon juice depending on how tangy you like the sauce. Add more lemon juice for more tang

You can make your Baba Ganoush several days ahead and store in the refrigerator until ready to serve

SUCCOT

Butternut Squash Soup

V,GF

In New England, the harvest of butternut squash is synonymous with the welcoming of the beautiful fall weather and vibrant foliage. Butternut squash is a vegetable that takes us straight through winter so we're always able to have a colorful, nutritious bowl of soup on the table.

Serves 8-10

INGREDIENTS

2 tbsp coconut oil or extra virgin olive oil

1 large butternut squash, roasted whole for 1 hour at 375°F

1 head of fennel, roughly chopped

3 cups kale, tough stalks removed & roughly chopped

2 green apples, peeled & roughly chopped

2" piece of ginger, peeled & chopped

½ large Vidalia onion, peeled & roughly chopped

4-5 cups vegetable stock (depends how much water content is in your squash and how thick/thin you like your soup)

3 cloves garlic, smashed

2 tbsp cumin

1 tsp turmeric

½ cup roughly chopped fresh sage + additional whole sage for garnish

pumpkin seeds for garnish

salt & pepper to taste

INSTRUCTIONS

Roast butternut squash whole in preheated 375°F oven for one hour (it's okay if it's still a little firm as it will continue to cook in the broth). Let cool slightly, split horizontally, remove skin and seeds and roughly chop

Sauté onions on medium-low heat until translucent

Add fennel and ginger and cook about a minute until you start to smell the ginger

Add the garlic and spices and cook for another minute

Add kale, apples and cooked, chopped butternut squash and mix in with all the other ingredients

Add 4 cups stock, salt and pepper

Bring to a boil and let simmer for 20 minutes

Taste and adjust seasoning as needed

Stir in fresh chopped sage

Purée soup in blender or with immersion blender. Add additional stock if soup is too thick

Serve garnished with pumpkin seeds and sage

NOTES

You can freeze butternut squash soup. When you're ready to eat it, just defrost in a pot on the stove over a low heat.

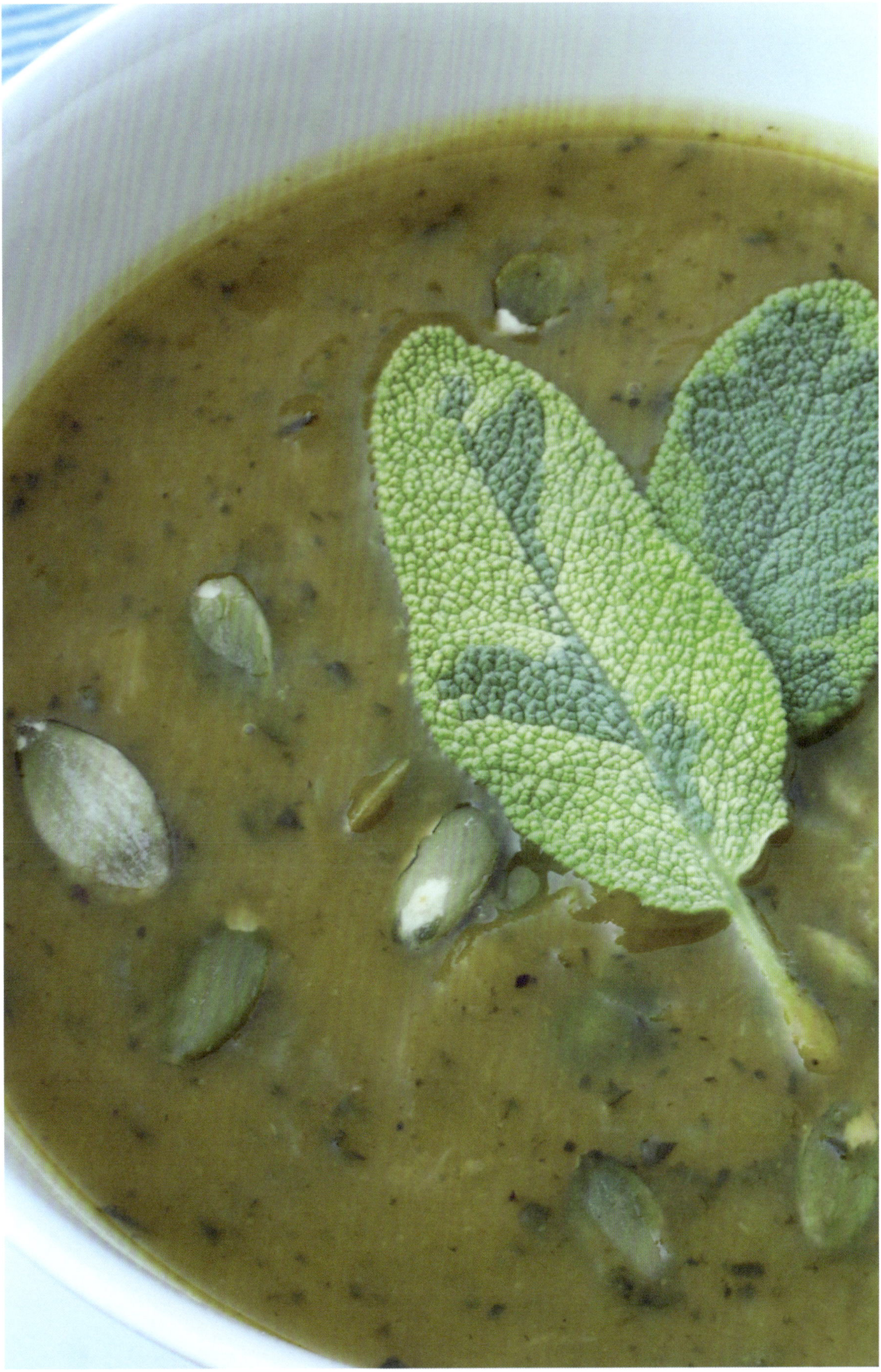

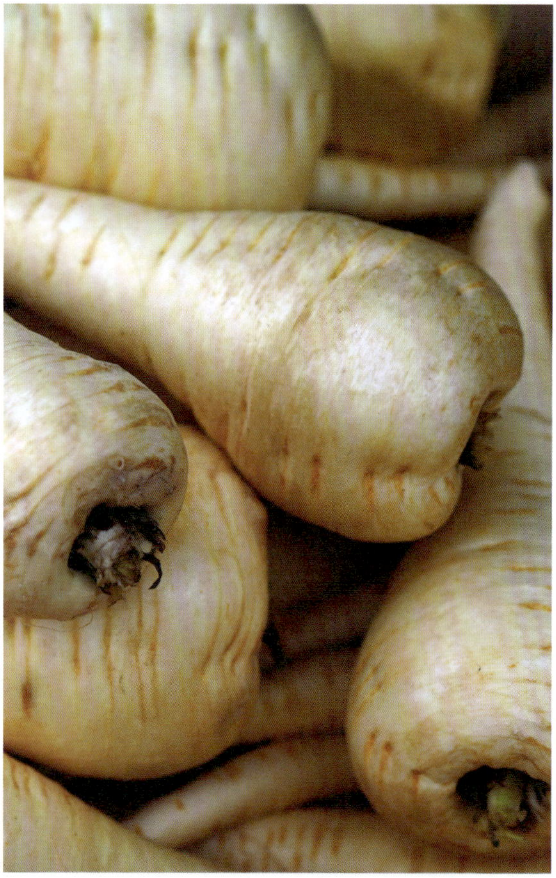
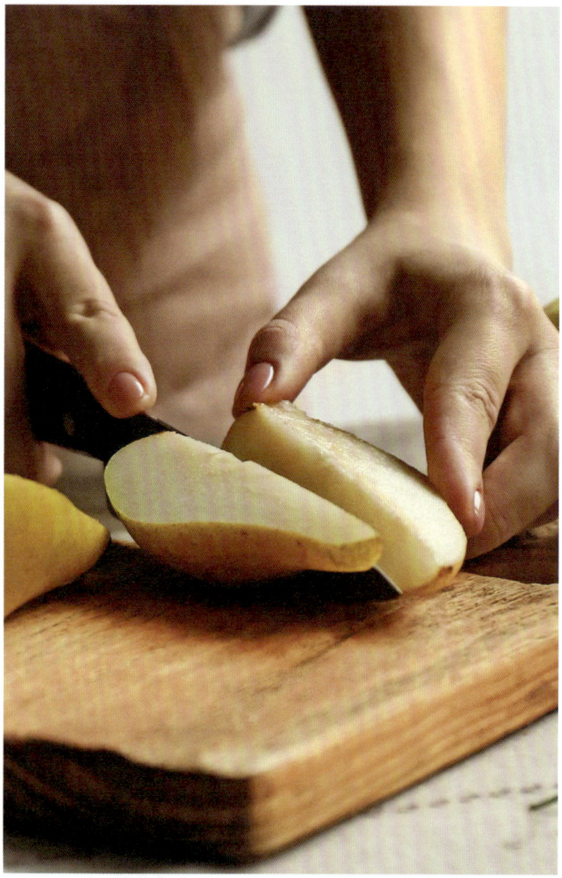
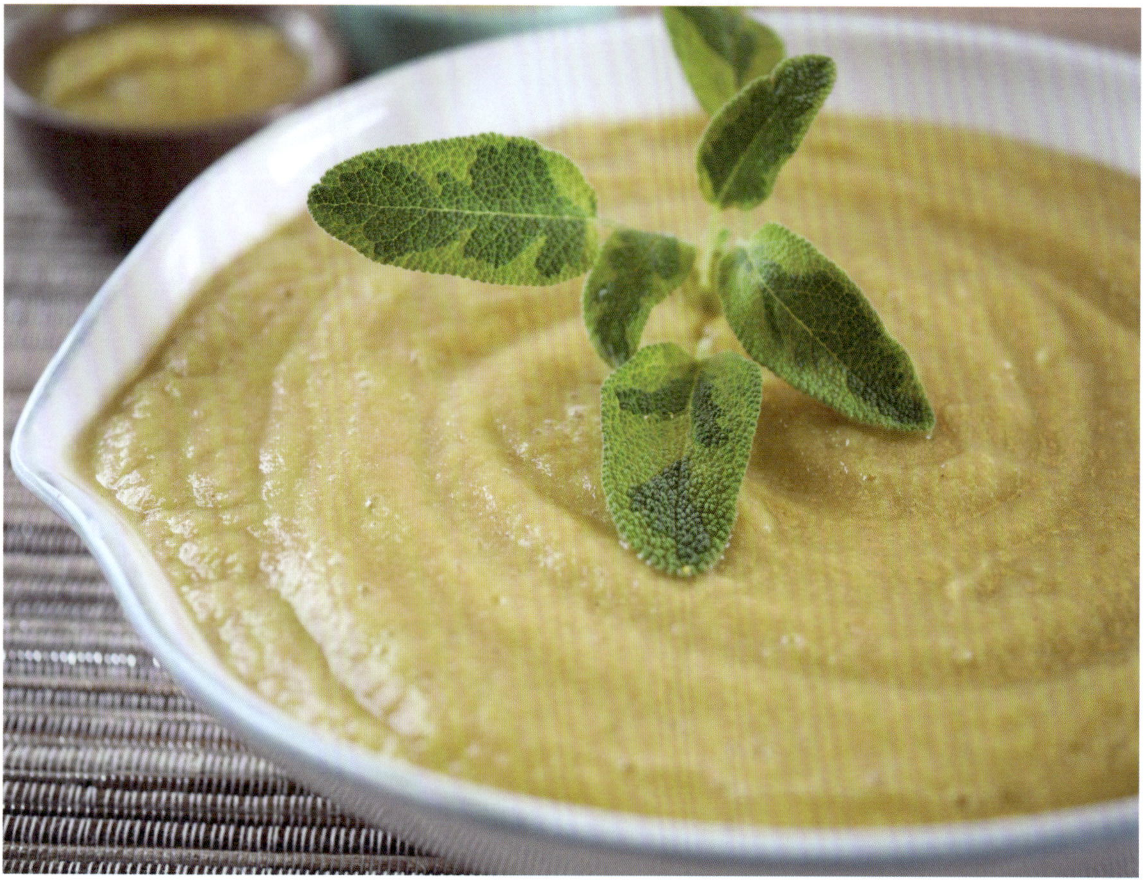

Parsnip and Apple Soup

V,GF

—

This is a satisfying soup that will brighten your table anytime. Easy-to-make and freezes well so be sure to put some in the freezer and you'll have something healthy to heat up in minutes.

Serves 8-10 appetizer portions

INGREDIENTS

2 tbsp coconut oil or extra virgin olive oil

1 medium onion or ½ large onion, peeled & roughly chopped

1 clove garlic, peeled & roughly chopped

2 parsnips, peeled & roughly chopped

1 apple, peeled & roughly chopped

1 pear, peeled & roughly chopped

1 carrot, peeled & roughly chopped

1 inch ginger, peeled & diced

3 cups vegetable stock

1 tsp cumin

1 tsp coriander

½ tsp turmeric

2-3 sprigs of sage, stems removed (plus extra for garnish)

3-4 sprigs of thyme, stems removed

salt & pepper to taste

INSTRUCTIONS

Put a large stockpot or enamel pot over medium heat and add coconut oil

Add onions and sauté until translucent

Add garlic and cook for about a minute

Add in the spices and stir until you can smell their aroma (about 1-2 minutes)

Put chopped parsnip, apple, pear, carrot and ginger in the pan. Cook on medium-low for about 5 minutes, stirring frequently, to meld all the flavors together

Add vegetable stock, salt and pepper and bring to a boil. Lower heat, cover and simmer for about 15 minutes more (until fruit and vegetables are soft enough to purée)

Stir in fresh herbs and adjust seasoning if necessary

Purée soup in blender (only fill about ¾ of the way up — do in batches if necessary) or with an immersion blender

Fattoush Salad

Although traditionally Lebanese in origin, Fattoush Salad is very common throughout the Middle East. It's a family style salad you can really dig into. Chock full of delicious ingredients and textures and topped with crunchy balsamic pita chips. We serve this at pretty much any occasion where we have a large crowd to feed and it's a healthy, delicious addition to our Succot feast.

Serves 8-10

INGREDIENTS

FOR THE SALAD

4 bundles romaine lettuce, washed, dried & chopped

2 English cucumbers, peeled & chopped

4 large tomatoes, chopped

¼ cup red onion, finely chopped

¼ cup dill pickles, chopped

¼ cup sweet gherkin pickles, chopped

½ cup pepperoncini, chopped

½ cup pomegranate seeds

2 cups feta cheese, crumbled

½ cup kalamata olives, pitted

¼ cup pine nuts, lightly toasted

¼ cup fresh mint, chopped

FOR THE DRESSING

1 cup olive oil

¼ cup balsamic vinegar

juice of 1 lemon

½ cup kalamata olives, pitted

2 garlic cloves

1 tbsp cumin

½ tsp salt

pepper to taste

FOR THE TOPPING

2 cups pita chips, crushed

½ cup balsamic glaze (available in the vinegar and olive oil section in your grocery store)

INSTRUCTIONS

Toss all salad ingredients in a large bowl and set aside

Place all dressing ingredients in a food processor or blender and purée

Combine crushed pita chips with balsamic glaze and set aside for 15-20 minutes

Right before serving, drizzle dressing over the salad and toss

Top with balsamic pita chips

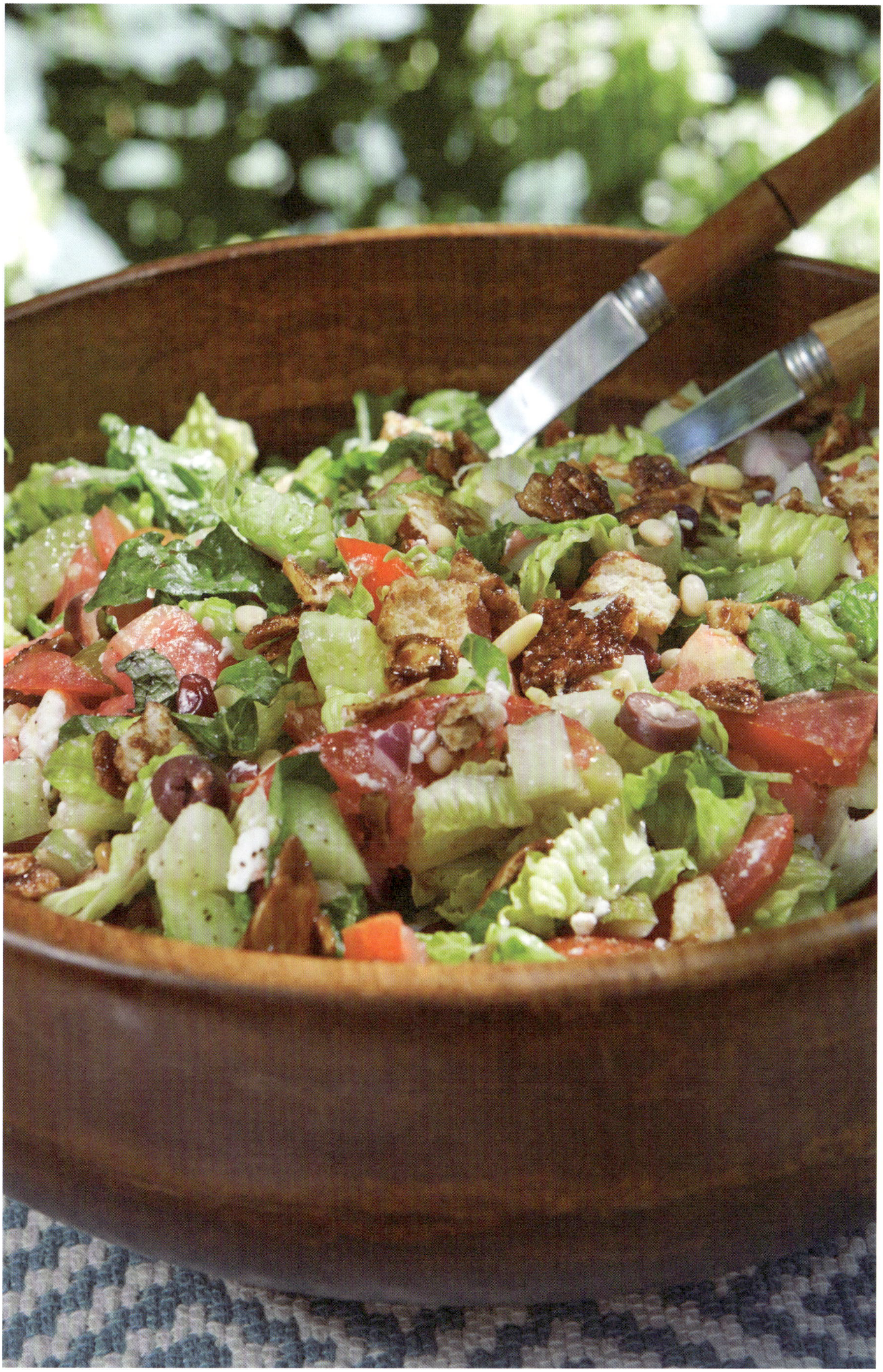

Tabbouleh

A Lebanese classic that we can't get enough of, Tabbouleh is a tasty addition to your Succot celebration or your Shabbat luncheon. It's also vegan. Scoop it up with romaine lettuce and simply enjoy, serve it as a side with your favorite entree or put some in a Pita pocket with Kafta and Tahini Sauce.

Serves 6-8

INGREDIENTS

¼ cup fine bulgur, rinsed

⅔ cup fresh lemon juice

2-3 medium tomatoes, finely chopped & drained (about 3 cups)

4 cups fresh parsley, chopped

½ cup fresh mint, finely chopped

½ cup red onion, finely chopped

2 tbsp olive oil

1 tsp cumin

1 tsp salt

pepper to taste

romaine leaves for serving

INSTRUCTIONS

Add bulgur and lemon juice to a bowl, stir together and let sit until bulgur has absorbed the lemon juice (about 5 minutes)

Add your chopped tomatoes, parsley, mint and red onion to the bulgur

Add cumin, salt and pepper, drizzle in olive oil and toss

Plate with romaine lettuce leaves which can be used as a serving device for the Tabbouleh

The tomatoes will continue to generate liquid when you assemble the salad so if you want to avoid too much juice in the bottom of your salad bowl, keep the salad in a strainer until serving

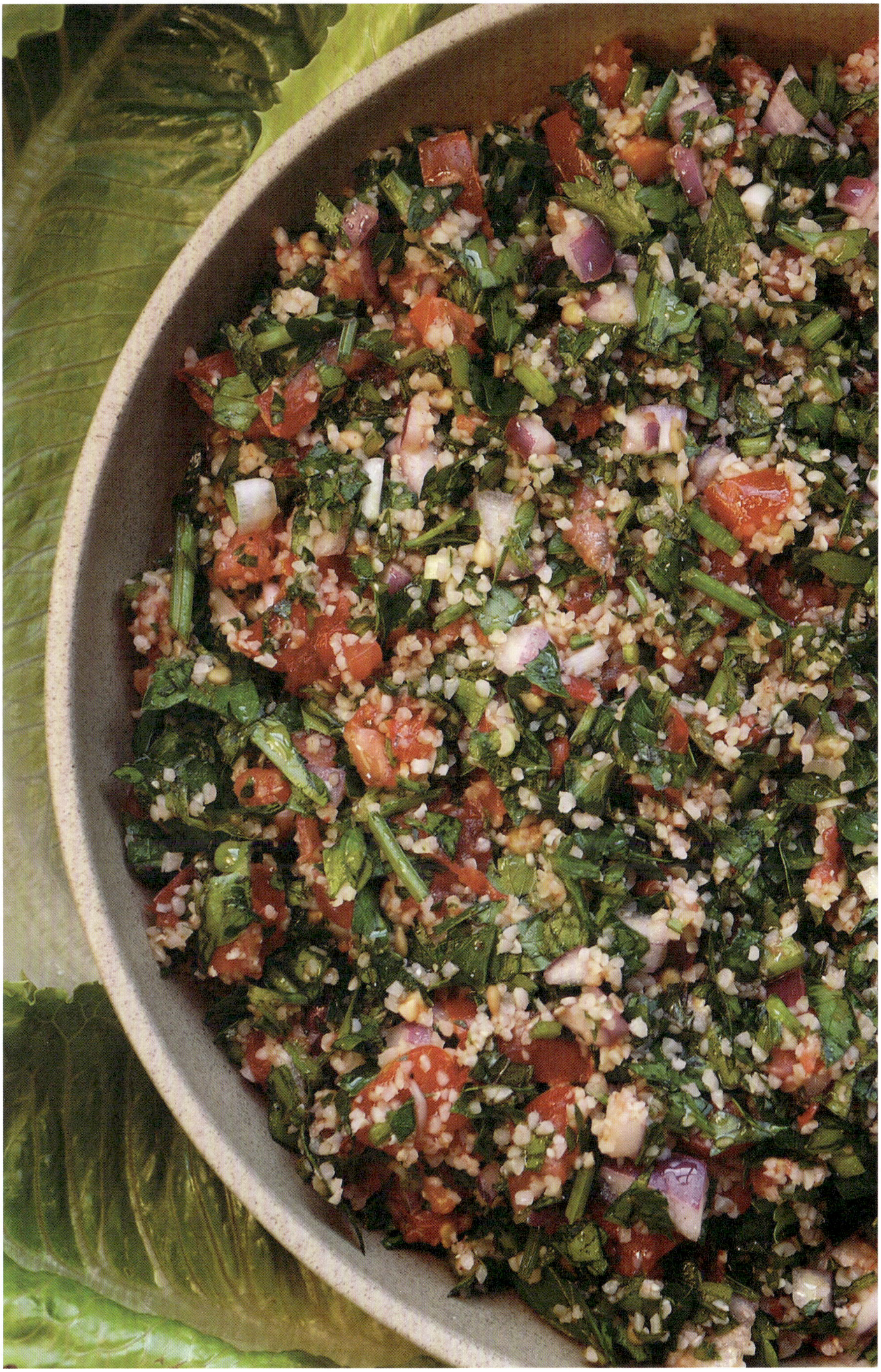

Shakshuka

—

I have always loved Shakshuka. It is such a delicious and healthy breakfast. On a trip to Israel, I realized we NEEDED to add Shakshuka to Breaking Matzo. I went for a walk on the beach and stopped at a seaside restaurant. I ordered Shakshuka and when I looked at the dish on my table and the Mediterranean only steps away, I knew that the time had come to bring this recipe to Breaking Matzo.

This Tunisian dish is perfect for breakfast, lunch or dinner. Typically served family style, you can also make individual portions which look beautiful on the table. The spicy tomato sauce can be made well in advance so you can simply heat, drop in your eggs, toast some bread and you're ready to serve.

SUCCOT

Shakshuka

GF

Serves 4

INGREDIENTS

¼ cup olive oil

5-6 eggs

1 large onion, peeled & finely chopped

5 lbs of your favorite tomatoes (we used a mix of heirloom and cherry tomatoes), roughly chopped (you can leave cherry tomatoes whole)

2 cloves garlic, peeled & minced

1 hot pepper — jalapeño, habanero, etc. (the more seeds you leave in, the spicier the dish)

1 cup of your favorite mushrooms, diced

1 large roasted red pepper (buy in a jar or roast a fresh pepper in broiler or on grill, remove charred skin, devein and chop into bite-size pieces)

1 tbsp smoked paprika

1 tbsp za'atar (an Israeli thyme, sumac and sesame seed blend available at specialty stores and online)

1 tsp cumin

pinch of cayenne pepper

2-3 sprigs of fresh thyme

salt & pepper to taste

INSTRUCTIONS

Heat a wide, heavy-bottomed skillet or Dutch oven on medium-low heat and add olive oil

Add onions to pan and sauté until they become translucent

Mix salt, pepper and other spices in with onions until spices are fragrant (about 1 minute)

Add garlic, let cook for 1-2 minutes. Watch carefully so it doesn't burn

Add mushrooms and hot pepper — sauté for another minute or so

Add tomatoes and roasted peppers to pan and cook on medium-low for 20-30 minutes until tomatoes have broken down and sauce has thickened a little (sauce may seem watery but it will set up once you take it off the stove for a few minutes)

Add more salt and pepper if needed

At this point, you could let the sauce cool and put it in the refrigerator or freezer until you are ready to use it. But if you want to make your Shakshuka right away, crack the eggs right into the heated sauce in the pan, spacing them apart from each other

Cover the pan with a lid and let eggs poach on low heat for about 8 minutes, occasionally basting the whites with the sauce. The eggs are done when the whites are opaque

Adjust seasoning if needed

Garnish with fresh thyme and serve family style with crusty bread

NOTES

You can also make individual Shakshuka servings using small ramekins. It's a slightly different process. Spoon some of the heated sauce into the ramekins and crack 1 egg into each ramekin. Place the ramekins on a cookie sheet and put under the broiler for 2-4 minutes, until the eggs have set up to your liking.

SUCCOT

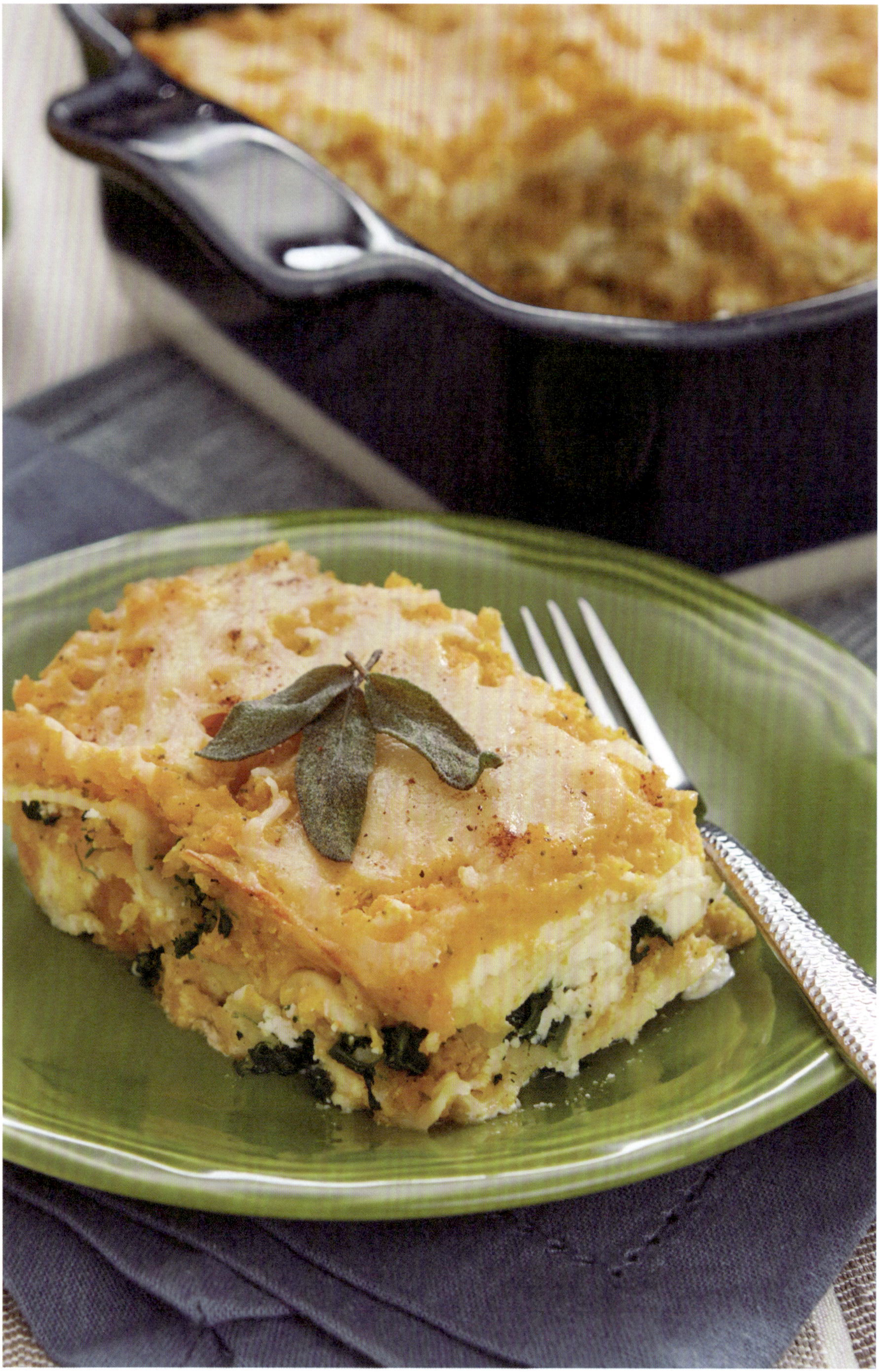

Butternut Squash Lasagna

The Succot holiday celebrates the fall harvest and nothing says fall harvest better than butternut squash. We created this vegetarian lasagna recipe for the spread we make for our family and friends. We love to cook with fresh local ingredients and butternut squash is plentiful in New England in the fall. Not only does the classic combination of squash and sage taste delicious but the bright orange color looks beautiful on your table. This recipe is also an ideal vegetarian option for your Bar/Bat Mitzvah menu.

Serves 10-12

INGREDIENTS

1 box lasagna noodles (1 lb, pre-cooked dried if possible)

2 medium-sized butternut squash (roasted, peeled, seeds removed & rough chopped — about 8 cups. Or you can buy already prepped at the supermarket)

1 cup fresh sage

2 tbsp honey

1 lb frozen spinach, defrosted & water squeezed out

1 cup mascarpone cheese

3 cups fresh mozzarella cheese, grated

2 cups parmesan cheese, grated (½ cup for ricotta mixture, 1-½ cups to sprinkle over layers)

2 quarts ricotta cheese (two containers)

1 egg, lightly beaten

2 tsp salt

pepper to taste

INSTRUCTIONS

PREPARE LASAGNA COMPONENTS

Preheat oven to 375°F

Roast butternut squash whole for 1 hour or until you can easily pierce with a knife

Meanwhile, in a mixing bowl combine the ricotta cheese, ½ cup parmesan cheese and egg

Set aside

When squash is cooked, let cool slightly, cut in half horizontally, peel, remove the seeds and roughly chop

Place squash, mascarpone, sage, honey, salt and pepper in a food processor or blender and pulse, leaving some chunks of squash for texture

LAYER THE LASAGNA

In a 3 quart or 4.8 quart lasagna pan, make layers of butternut squash purée, spinach, ricotta mixture, parmesan, mozzarella and lasagna sheets until pan is full (3-4 layers). Do not put mozzarella on the top of lasagna until it has baked for 45 minutes covered with aluminum foil. Then add mozzarella and bake uncovered for an additional 15 minutes or until mozzarella is melted and slightly brown

Let cool for 30 minutes before cutting slices

NOTES

You can assemble the lasagna a day ahead and refrigerate unbaked. Or you can bake, let cool, refrigerate and reheat. Lasagna tastes even better the next day.

Quinoa and Vegetable Stuffed Acorn Squash

V, GF

Bring fall to the table with quinoa and vegetable stuffed squash. Don't forget to tell your guests to scrape the inside of the squash along with the other ingredients to fully enjoy the dish. This recipe also works very well with mini pumpkins such as the sugar pie variety.

Serves 6-8

INGREDIENTS

6-8 acorn squash

2 tbsp coconut oil

2 cups quinoa, cooked according to package instructions

1 large onion, finely chopped

1 cup fennel, finely chopped

2 cups shiitake mushrooms, finely chopped

4 carrots, peeled & finely chopped

2 red bell peppers, finely chopped

2 cups fresh tomato, finely chopped

2 tbsp ginger, peeled & minced or grated

5 cloves garlic, minced

1 red chile pepper, chopped (remove seeds if you want to reduce spiciness)

3 tbsp fresh thyme, stems removed & roughly chopped just before adding to dish

3 tbsp coconut aminos (or gluten-free soy sauce)

¾ cup vegetable stock

juice of 1 lemon

2 tbsp cumin

salt & pepper to taste

INSTRUCTIONS

PREPARE SQUASH

Preheat oven to 375°F

Cut "lids" off the squash and remove seeds

Rub inside with olive oil and salt and roast squash and the lids on a parchment-lined cookie sheet for 1 hour or until you can easily pierce the base of the squash with a knife

Set cooked squash aside

PREPARE FILLING

Heat a large cast iron pan or Dutch oven on medium heat

Add coconut oil to the pan

When almost sizzling, add onion and turn heat down to medium-low

Cook onions until they are translucent

Add cumin, carrots and fennel and sauté for 2 minutes

Add garlic and ginger and cook for about a minute

Add tomatoes, mushrooms, red pepper and chile pepper and sauté for 2-3 minutes (remember, all these ingredients will bake again in the oven so they don't have to be completely cooked through at this stage)

Add coconut aminos and vegetable stock; stir into the filling and let the liquid evaporate (2-4 minutes)

Season with salt and pepper to taste then stir in fresh thyme, lemon juice and cooked quinoa

STUFF SQUASH & BAKE

Preheat oven to 350°F

Spoon filling into each squash; top with lids

If filling is hot, bake for 15 minutes. If filling has been made ahead and refrigerated, bake for 30-40 minutes until filling is warmed through

Serve immediately or at room temperature

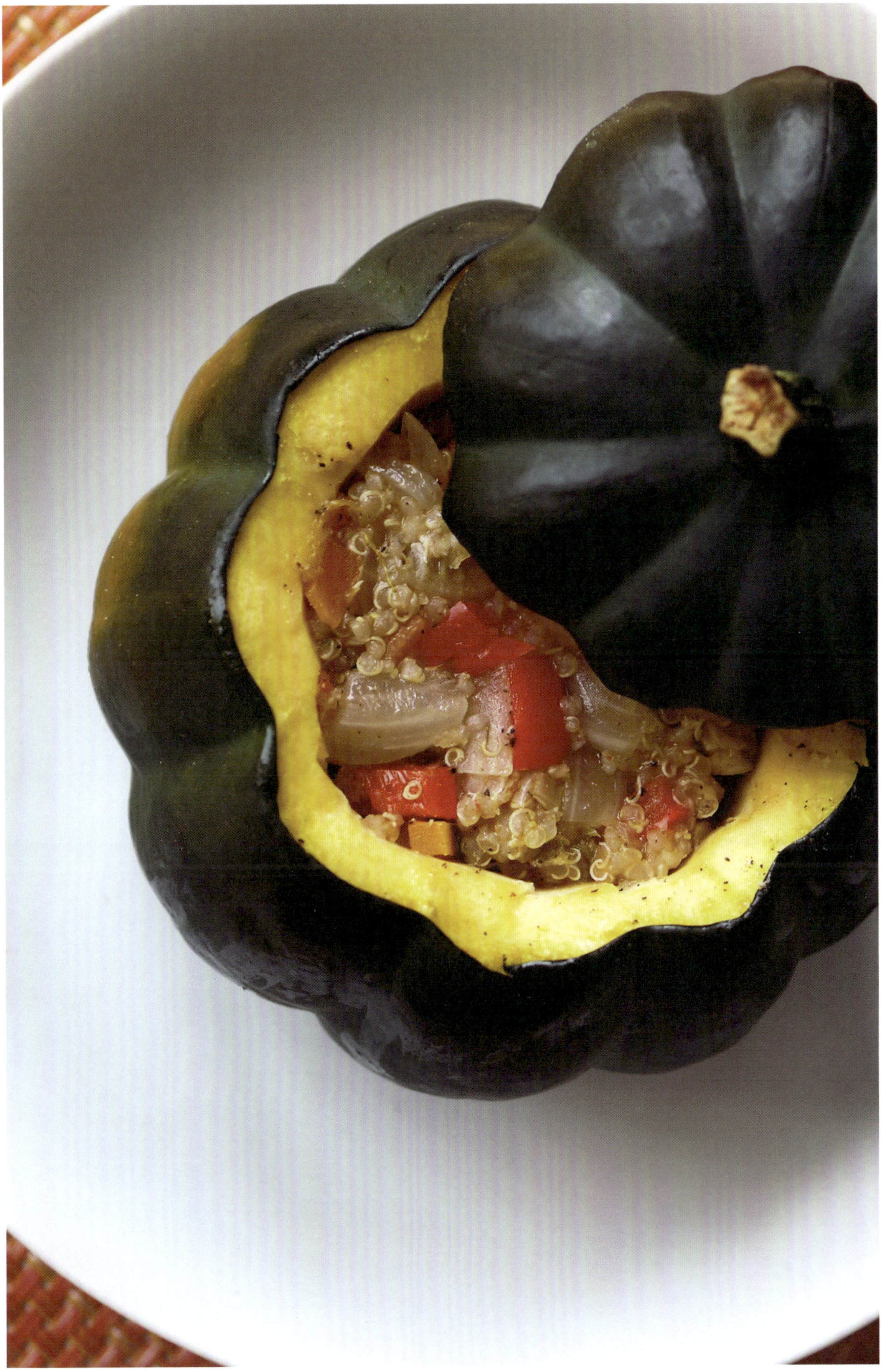

Moroccan Inspired Vegan Stuffed Artichokes

V, GF

These Moroccan Inspired Vegan Stuffed Artichokes are very versatile in that they can be served warm, room temperature or even chilled. Perfect as an appetizer or turn it into a meal with a nice side salad. Vegan or not, everyone loves this light, healthy dish. Try it for Succot or Shabbat.

Makes 4 Large Stuffed Artichokes

INGREDIENTS

4 large artichokes

¾ cup quinoa

1-¼ cup vegetable stock (or water)

2 tbsp olive oil + extra for drizzling on top of artichokes

1 onion, finely diced

1 clove garlic, minced

1 tbsp fresh ginger, peeled & grated

1 lemon, sliced

1 cup fresh parsley, chopped

½ cup fresh mint, finely chopped

½ cup nutritional yeast

½ tsp apple cider vinegar

kosher salt & pepper to taste

3 tbsp pine nuts, toasted

dry white wine (enough to fill your pan 1")

INSTRUCTIONS

MAKE FILLING

Rinse and strain quinoa

Add vegetable stock (or water) to a sauce pan and bring to a simmer

Stir in quinoa and simmer covered for 15 minutes

Fluff with a fork and pour into a bowl so it doesn't overcook. Set aside

Heat a skillet on medium heat and add olive oil

Sauté onion on medium-low until soft and translucent

Add garlic and ginger to pan and sauté for 1 minute

Add parsley, mint, salt and pepper and mix well for about 1 minute

Take off heat and stir in pine nuts, nutritional yeast & apple cider vinegar

Add all ingredients to the bowl of cooked quinoa and toss

Set aside

PREP ARTICHOKES

Fill a large bowl with water and squeeze the juice of the lemon slices into the bowl. Add the slices to the bowl

Cut off pointy tops of outer leaves of the artichokes with scissors (they are sharp and may give you splinters)

Peel off tough outer leaves — usually 2-3 layers. Use gloves if you want to protect your hands

Spread out the leaves of the artichoke with your hands and make an opening in the middle with your thumbs

Remove fuzzy choke in the middle with a spoon (dig deep — this takes some muscle)

Trim bottom of artichoke and make sure it has a flat surface so it will sit up straight in the pan

Submerge artichokes in the lemon water until ready to fill

FILL ARTICHOKES & BRAISE

Fill middle of artichokes and between leaves with quinoa filling

Drizzle a little olive oil on top of each

Place in a 4-quart pot with lemon slices and fill pot 1" with wine

Bring to a simmer, cover and braise for 40 minutes or until you can insert a knife easily into the base of the artichokes

Spaghetti Squash With Basil and Kale Pesto

V, GF

Who put the spaghetti in spaghetti squash? With a natural spaghetti texture that holds sauce almost as well as the finest Italian pasta, we don't know why this squash exists but we are grateful. If you are gluten intolerant or just prefer a vegetable to pasta with your sauces, spaghetti squash is the perfect alternative.

Serves 8

INGREDIENTS

3 large spaghetti squash, cut in half lengthwise (1 large spaghetti squash yields about 2-½ - 3 cups "spaghetti")

1 cup walnuts, lightly toasted in oven or on stovetop

4 cups of packed fresh basil + extra for garnish

2 cups of kale, stems removed

2 cloves garlic, roughly chopped

juice of 1 lemon

½ cup extra virgin olive oil

salt & pepper to taste

2 packages of frozen peas, warmed on stove and strained

6-8 cherry tomatoes, quartered

¼ cup Rawmesan (or pulse in a food processor — your favorite nuts, sesame seeds, nutritional yeast, dried herbs and salt), + extra for garnish

INSTRUCTIONS

Preheat the oven to 350°F

Roast the squash whole for 1 to 1-½ hours at 350°F or until you can insert a knife very easily in the flesh

While the squash is cooking, make pesto by putting the walnuts, basil, kale, garlic, lemon juice, Rawmesan, salt and pepper in a food processor and purée (you may need to do this in batches). While machine is going, drizzle in olive oil until your pesto has a nice smooth consistency. Taste and add more salt and pepper if needed

When squash are ready, cut each one in half lengthwise, remove the seeds and flake the "spaghetti" out with a fork

Toss the spaghetti squash with the pesto. For even distribution, spoon in a few tablespoons of pesto at a time

Make individual plates of the spaghetti squash and pesto mixture and sprinkle a little more Rawmesan and pepper on top (you can also serve a family style platter)

Garnish with a few fresh cherry tomato wedges, some peas and a sprig of fresh basil

NOTES

This dish can be served hot or room temperature.

SUCCOT

Apple Honey Cake

Celebrate Succot or Rosh Hashanah with a cake worthy of a special occasion. This Apple Honey Cake has an added surprise — a buttery, crumbly layer of streusel right through the middle. It's an extra special treat for family and friends.

Serves 8-10

INGREDIENTS

FOR CAKE BATTER

2 sticks butter, melted + 1 tbsp, melted for greasing the pan

3-½ cups all-purpose flour + extra for the pan

1 cup granulated sugar

½ cup light brown sugar, lightly packed

1 cup raw honey

3 large eggs

4 Granny Smith apples — 2 peeled & finely chopped; 2 peeled & puréed (or substitute 1-½ cups apple sauce for the 2 apples)

zest & juice of 1 lemon

1 tsp vanilla extract

1 tbsp baking powder

1 tsp baking soda

1 tbsp cinnamon

1 tsp kosher salt

½ cup pomegranate juice

FOR STREUSEL LAYER

¾ cup flour

¾ cup light brown sugar

2 tsp cinnamon

¼ cup butter, chopped into small cubes

¼ cup walnuts, chopped (optional)

FOR ICING

1-¾ cups confectioners sugar

¼ cup lemon juice

zest of 1 lemon (or more!)

INSTRUCTIONS

MAKE STREUSEL

Combine all ingredients in a small bowl and mix with your hands until it forms a crumbly mixture

Set aside

MAKE CAKE BATTER AND LAYER WITH STREUSEL

Preheat the oven to 350°F

Brush a bundt cake pan with melted butter, making sure you coat every crevice so the cake doesn't stick to the pan, then sprinkle a little flour all around the pan and turn it to coat evenly. Tip extra flour that hasn't adhered to the butter out of the pan

Sift your dry ingredients — flour, baking powder, baking soda, cinnamon and salt. Set aside

In a small bowl, combine the apple purée with the pomegranate juice. Set aside

Using a stand mixer or hand mixer, mix the melted butter, granulated sugar, honey, brown sugar, eggs, lemon juice, lemon zest and vanilla on medium speed until smooth (a minute or so)

With the mixer on low, add the flour mixture from Step 3 in thirds. Scrape down the bowl in between to ensure the batter is well combined

Add in the apple purée and pomegranate juice mixture and mix just until combined

Fold in your chopped apples

Pour HALF the batter into the buttered bundt pan

Evenly distribute the streusel layer in the middle of the cake batter then pour in the rest of the batter and smooth out completely covering the streusel

Bake for 75-85 minutes or until a knife comes out clean when inserted into the cake (ovens vary)

Let cool for 10 minutes in the pan, loosen the edges gently with a round-edged knife and invert onto a cake stand or plate (use potholders — pan will still be hot). Let completely cool before icing or icing will melt

MAKE ICING AND ICE CAKE

With a hand or stand mixer, mix all ingredients together until smooth. Icing should be fairly thick so that it will coat the cake nicely and slowly drip down the edges

If you'd like to keep your cake stand nice and tidy while you decorate, insert pieces of parchment paper under the cake which you can pull out once you're done icing the cake

Spoon icing into a vessel with a spout (a flexible silicone measuring cup works great) and slowly pour the icing over the top of the entire cake in a clockwise motion (or use a cake stand and turn the stand)

Gently encourage the icing to drip down the sides with a spoon or offset spatula if necessary

Slice and serve

NOTES

Cake will stay fresh for 2-3 days. Be sure to cover with plastic wrap and add icing the day you will be serving it.

Apple Rose

Pastries

Whether celebrating the abundance of Succot, Rosh Hashanah or a Bar/Bat Mitzvah, these beautiful stuffed Apple Rose Pastries are made extra magical with the addition of almond paste. Make these with the family and take turns rolling the dough, laying down the apple slices and rolling up the pastry.

SUCCOT

Apple Rose Pastries

Makes 4-5 Apple Rose Pastries per sheet of puff pastry

INGREDIENTS

1 package frozen puff pastry sheets (there are 2 sheets in a Pepperidge Farm package)

flour for rolling out pastry sheets

2 red apples

1 13-oz jar of our Etrog Marmalade or orange marmalade

1 7-oz package of almond paste

1 cup sugar

1 tbsp cinnamon

juice of 1 lemon

water for partially cooking the apple slices and thinning out jam/marmalade

INSTRUCTIONS

Preheat to 375°F

PREP

Butter a muffin tin or ramekins

Thaw puff pastry sheets per package instructions

While puff pastry is thawing, mix cinnamon and sugar in a bowl and set aside

Spoon marmalade in a bowl and stir in a little water so it's easy to spread on the pastry (have a pastry brush or spoon handy)

Add water and lemon juice to a medium size bowl (enough to cover the apple slices)

Cut 2 apples in half and remove cores. Thinly slice the apple halves (almost paper thin). Do not peel apples. The red color is what gives the pastry the red rose color

Place slices of apple in the lemon water so they don't brown

Microwave apples for about 2-4 minutes so they are bendable and won't break when rolled. You can also cook the apples on the stovetop in lemon water for 3-5 minutes. Strain apples, pat dry and spread out so you can easily pick them up and layer them on the pastry dough

Flour your work surface and roll out a sheet of pastry. Cut 4-5 vertical strips about 10" long. Cover the ones you are not currently working on with a damp towel so they don't dry out

ASSEMBLY

For each strip, brush with marmalade

Sprinkle a generous amount of cinnamon-sugar over the entire strip

On the right side of the strip, overlay your apple slices so the red rounded edge of the slices are facing out

To the left of the apple slices, add little pads of flattened almond paste

Fold the left side of the strip over the pads of almond paste (about 1")

Roll up the strip and place in a buttered muffin tin or ramekin

Repeat and bake roses for 30 minutes at 375°F then adjust heat to 350°F and bake for another 20 minutes

Remove from tins (you may need a round-edged knife to loosen them from the pan or ramekin). Best served warm

NOTES

Almond paste is available online, in specialty stores and better supermarkets.

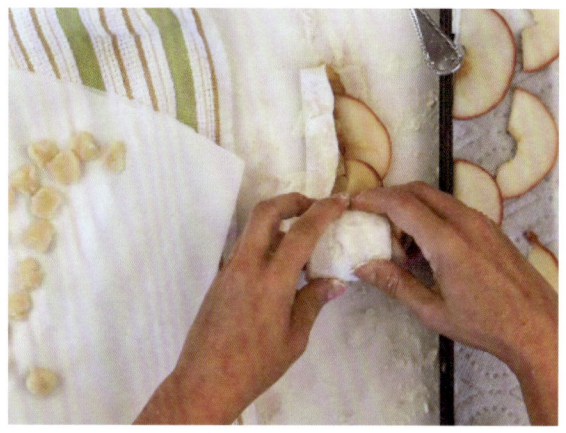

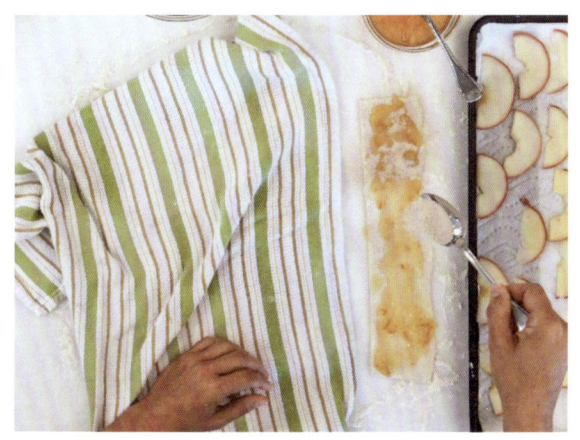

SUCCOT

115

V, GF

Vanilla and Anise Poached Pears

Pears are plentiful in the fall. And there are so many varieties, from Bartlett to Bosc. Pears are typically poached in a simple syrup but we wanted to showcase the natural sweetness of the fruit and make a healthier dessert so we use a little water and some fragrant whole spices and herbs in this version. We also made this a non-dairy dessert and use coconut yogurt instead of milk-based yogurt or ice cream. If you have leftovers, you can slice the pears thin and add them to salads.

Serves 8

INGREDIENTS

4 firm pears (Bosc recommended), peeled, cored & halved

just enough water to cover the pears

1 vanilla bean

2 cinnamon sticks

4-5 star anise

1 large sprig of fresh rosemary

coconut yogurt or whipped full fat canned coconut milk for garnish

cinnamon for garnish

chopped nuts or toasted unsweetened coconut for garnish

INSTRUCTIONS

Split the vanilla bean with a paring knife and scrape the seeds out. Add them to a large pot along with the whole vanilla pod

Place pears in the pot with the rest of the ingredients and pour enough water just to cover the ingredients

Simmer covered until you can pierce the pears easily with a knife (10-20 minutes depending on the firmness of the pears so keep an eye on them)

Remove from heat and serve half a pear per person with a dollop of whipped coconut milk or coconut yogurt, cinnamon and chopped nuts. You can also spoon your yogurt or whipped whole fat canned coconut milk in a bowl and sit the pear on top along with some chopped nuts or toasted coconut

NOTES

You can make the pears ahead and store in the liquid a day or two before serving. Reheat pears in the liquid on the stove before serving.

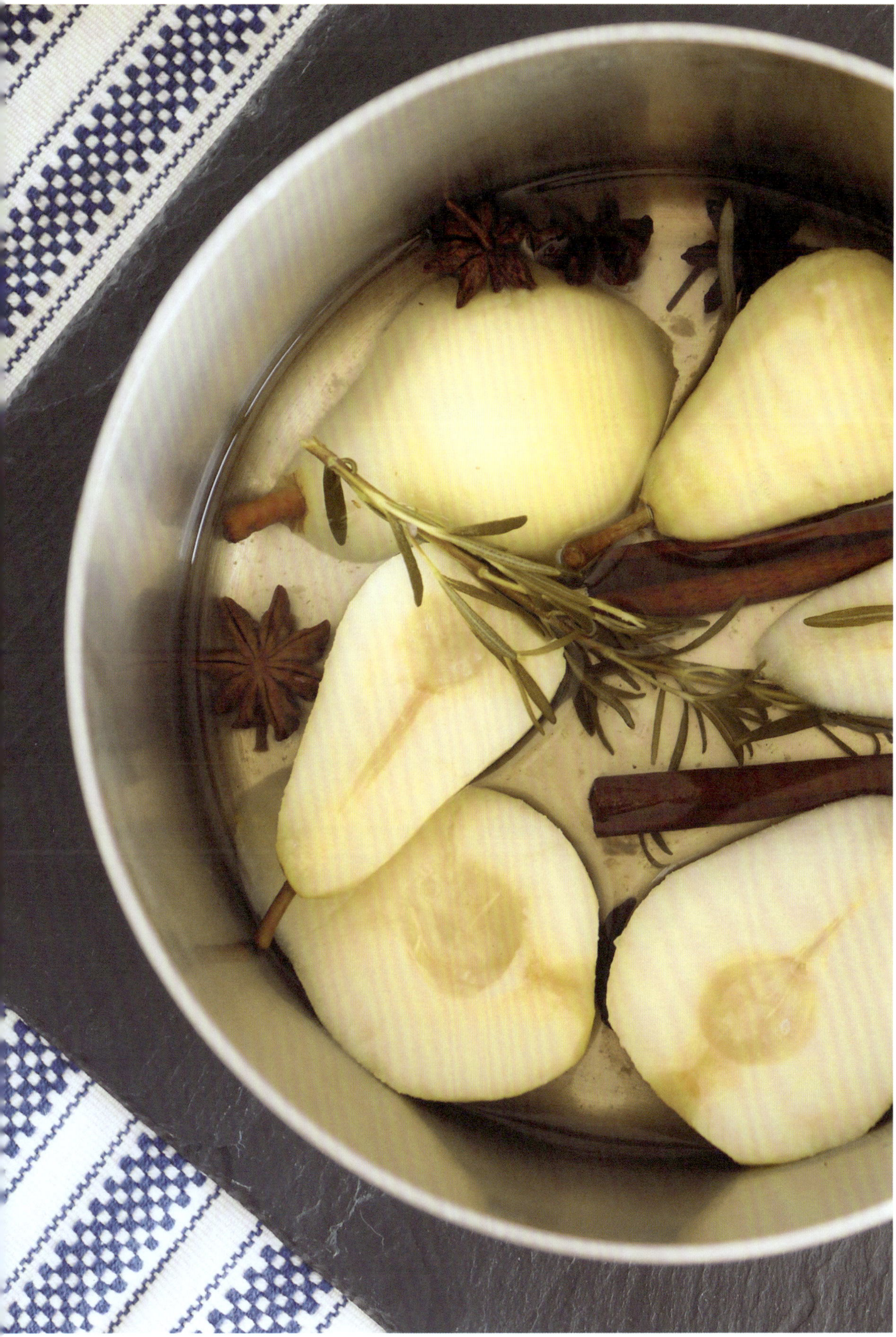

Apple Cider Hot Toddy

Here's something warm to sip in your succah when there's a fall chill in the air. This recipe is a combination of a hot toddy and mulled cider since we steep warm spices in the cider. We think it makes the beverage extra appealing — smells amazing and tastes even better. We added apple cider and apple brandy in celebration of Succot. Omit the apple brandy and bourbon for a non-alcoholic version that the kids can enjoy.

Serves 4

INGREDIENTS

2-½ cups apple cider

1 cup freshly brewed black tea (Irish or English breakfast)

6 oz bourbon (we love Mad River Distillers, made by our friends from Vermont)

2 oz apple brandy

3 lemons (1 for steeping, 1 for squeezing into drinks, 1 for garnish)

1 vanilla bean

1 tbsp honey

4-5 whole cloves

5 cinnamon sticks (1 for steeping, 4 for garnish)

8 whole star anise (4 for steeping, 4 for garnish)

INSTRUCTIONS

Pour apple cider in a saucepan

Slice one of your lemons in quarters and add to pan

Split vanilla bean down the middle, remove seeds inside with a paring knife and place vanilla bean and seeds in the pan

Add honey, cloves, 1 cinnamon stick and 4 star anise to the pan

Bring cider to a boil then simmer for 20 minutes covered (after you turn off the stove, you can let the cider steep with the spices — the longer you let it steep, the more the spice flavors will permeate the cider)

Add tea to the steeped cider, strain and discard the spices (if you are making this ahead, keep the spices in and refrigerate)

To make each drink, add 1-½ oz of bourbon, ½ oz of apple brandy and a squeeze of a lemon wedge to a glass then fill the rest of the glass with your hot spiced apple cider/tea blend. (If you are making a non-alcoholic version, just leave out the bourbon and brandy)

Garnish each drink with a wheel of lemon, a cinnamon stick and a star anise (or just the lemon slice is fine as well)

NOTES

You can make the steeped cider a few days ahead of time and store in the refrigerator. Simply reheat and follow the assembly steps in the recipe to make each Hot Toddy.

SUCCOT

119

What Is Succot?

Succot is the Festival of Booths. It takes place in the fall four days after Yom Kippur. It is a seven-day holiday (eight days outside the Land of Israel), a time for communal celebration following the intensity of the High Holy Days and is a celebration of the harvest.

There are two traditional explanations to the origins of the holiday of Succot: the first is that the Israelites dwelt in succot after the Exodus from Egypt (Leviticus 23:42-43). According to one rabbinic sage, the wilderness succot (plural of succah) were not physical tents, but "Clouds of Glory" (Babylonian Talmud, Berachot 54b), special clouds God provided for the people to guide and protect them during their 40 years of wilderness wandering (see Exodus 13:21).

The second explanation for Succot is that once our ancestors arrived in the Land of Israel and lived an agricultural lifestyle, farmers built succot while gathering up their produce during the harvest season to maximize their productivity (Exodus 34:22). In fact, one of the names for the holiday is "The Festival of Ingathering."

In either case, Succot is a time for celebration and is referred to as "The Season of Our Joy." It is an occasion to give thanks for the bounty of life. Dwelling in a succah is also a sign of trust: even as the winter approaches, we trust that God will provide for us throughout the cold and dark months ahead. We sit in our makeshift booths, aware of our vulnerability, as an expression of our faith.

In addition to the Succah, the other significant ritual objects of Succot are the lulav and the etrog. Like most Jewish ceremonial items, the lulav (palm branch, myrtle, and willows) and the etrog (citron) have philosophical meanings. The ancient rabbis spent many hours discuss-ing and trying to interpret the words and meanings of each law. And through the centuries, they have handed down various interpretations of the symbolism of the lulav and the etrog.

One popular rabbinic teaching is that the four components of the lulav and the etrog, which are called in Hebrew the arba minim, symbolize the human condition and one's relationship with God. The etrog is shaped like the heart and the lulav like the spine. The myrtle leaves are shaped like the eyes and the willow leaves like the lips. Together these four elements show that one should serve God with his or her heart, spine or body, eyes and lips.

There is another symbolic layer of meaning related to the etrog and lulav and two forms of Jewish sacred action: study and good deeds. The etrog, which has a good taste and a good smell, is like those who know the Torah and do good deeds. While the lulav which has a good taste but no smell, is like a person with knowledge but who does no good deeds. The myrtle, which has a good smell and no taste, is like a simple person who has no knowledge and learning but is innately kind and caring. Lowest on the rung of human values is the willow, which has neither taste nor fragrance, and symbolizes those people with no interest in gaining knowledge, no innate sense of responsibility towards others and no feeling of the need to help others.

Each day during Succot, blessings are recited over the etrog and the lulav. The etrog is held in the left hand and the lulav in the right hand. The lulav is shaken in six directions (north, south, east, and west, up and down) to remind us that God is everywhere.

Further, while most Jewish holidays have agriculture roots, they are more widely known for their connections to their historical narratives. Shavuot (The Festival of Weeks), for example, was originally a celebration of the first fruits of the late spring harvest. Succot, however, has maintained a strong connection to the earth because of the central symbols of the holiday: the succah (temporary booth), and the *lulav* (palm branch, myrtle and willows) and *etrog* (citron). This fall holiday offers us the opportunity to reflect on the blessings of the natural world and our place in it.

Succot is immediately followed by the holidays of *Sh'mini Atzeret* and *Simchat Torah*. The former is designated as an additional day of "holy assembly," while the latter is a celebration (simchah = joy) of the completion of the annual cycle of Torah readings (Genesis through Deuteronomy).

Sukkos - 1973

Pictured clockwise from upper right: Dr. Ada Goldfarb - Andy's aunt, Rabbi Daniel Goldfarb — Andy's uncle, a family friend and Myra Yellin Goldfarb Outwater, Andy's mother, 1973

Most Jewish holidays celebrate God's miraculous intervention at specific moments in ancient Jewish history. For example, on Passover we recall how God freed Hebrew slaves from slavery in Egypt with the Ten Plagues and the Parting of the Sea of Reeds. And on Hanukkah, we remember God's support of Judah and his fellow Maccabees against the Syrian-Greek army, and the miraculous jug of oil the Maccabees discovered when they recaptured the Temple in Jerusalem. Succot, however, is a celebration of God's ongoing presence in the lives of our ancestors and in our lives today.

Scan for video

SUCCOT

Succot
Discussion Questions
—

1. **Succot is a time to rejoice and celebrate.**

    What do you want to celebrate in your life?

    Who would you like to celebrate with?

2. There are two classic explanations for the holiday of Succot. One is that the Children of Israel lived in succot while wandering in the wilderness before entering The Promised Land. The other is that they built temporary huts or booths during the fall harvest season once living in the Land of Israel ("succah of abundance").

    What is your "succah of abundance?"

    What do you have in abundance?

    How do you express your gratitude?

    What is your "succah of wilderness?"

    What do you have that is most precious?

    Where do you receive support when you feel most vulnerable?

For Kids

   What do you have a lot of? Does it make you happy?

   What do you have that is most precious?

   How would that change if you had a lot of it?

3. **Succot is a celebration of the fall harvest.**

    How do you celebrate? Apple picking? Gardening? Harvesting fall vegetables?

    How do you celebrate your life's bountiful occasions? Are there momentous events or milestones for which you are particularly proud? Do you have a loved one who has reached an important milestone? How do you celebrate their achievement?

4. The succah is a wonderful opportunity to celebrate with family, friends, neighbors and even new acquaintances.

   Who would you like to invite into your succah this year?

   Is there someone in your life that has passed away that you would like to join you in the succah this year?

   Is there an historical or literary figure you would like to invite into the succah? Why?

5. If possible, take the time to eat at least one meal with your family or friends in the succah this year. If you cannot sit in a succah, try a park or another beautiful outdoor space.

   How is this different from your usual meals? How does it feel eating a meal in the succah (or outdoors)?

6. Succot marks the transition from fall to winter as we celebrate the autumn harvest.

   How are you preparing for winter?

   What do you enjoy most about the fall?

7. As part of our Succot celebration, we hold the lulav and etrog in our hands and shake them in 6 directions: north, south, east, west, up, down to signify the divine presence that infuses all of life.

   Have you ever experienced God or the Divine Spirit in your life?

   Is there a particular place where you feel a sense of connection with life as a whole?

Hanukkah

APPETIZERS
Potato Latkes
Potato and Cheddar Latkes with Horseradish Sour Cream
Sweet Potato Latkes
Gluten-Free Zucchini Latkes
Marzipan Stuffed Dates

SIDES & SAUCES
Caroline's Apple Sauce
Andy's Meat Sauce

ENTREES
Za'atar Roast Chicken
Bubbie's Stuffed Cabbage
Chraime (Sephardic Fish Dish)
Classic Meatballs
Lentil Curry over Cauliflower Mash

Hanukkah is the Festival of Lights, a holiday which commemorates the rededication of the Holy Temple in Jerusalem from the Syrian-Greeks in 164 BCE by a small but mighty army led by Judah the Maccabee. We celebrate by lighting the Menorah for 8 nights which allows us to participate in the ongoing miracle of renewing the light of Judaism, generation to generation.

Many of the dishes we enjoy during Hanukkah are cooked in oil. Why? To remind us of the central Miracle of Oil, when the lamp oil needed for the Maccabees to light the Menorah lasted for eight days instead of burning out in only one. So lucky us, we get to load up on Latkes and dig into delicious Donuts!

DESSERTS
Sufganiyot (Jelly Donuts)
Loukoumades (Sephardic Greek Donuts)
Louisa's Kugel
Nana's Puff Pancake
Apple-Cinnamon Dessert Latkes
Gelt (Chocolate Coins)
Vegan Chocolate Pudding

V = Vegan
GF = Gluten Free

Potato Latkes

It's hard to top the excitement of making latkes for Hanukkah! The scent of the potatoes frying in oil, the crackle as they brown AND the crispy texture and savory flavor. For us, latke making is the Hanukkah holiday wrapped up in one delectable sensory experience. We celebrate the holiday by cooking food in oil to remind us of the central miracle of Hanukkah, when the lamp oil lasted for eight days instead of burning out in only one. Make a lot of potato latkes! At our family gatherings there are never any leftovers. We even eat the crumbs.

Makes 10-12 latkes

INGREDIENTS

LATKES

3 russet potatoes, peeled & grated

2 eggs, lightly beaten

½ onion, peeled & grated

1 carrot, peeled & grated

½ cup matzo meal or all-purpose flour

1 tsp salt

pepper to taste

vegetable oil for frying

CAROLINE'S LATKE SAUCE

1 16-oz container sour cream

1 tsp cumin

pinch of salt

INSTRUCTIONS

LATKES

Peel potatoes and onion and process with grating blade in food processor or grate by hand with box grater. Set aside

In large mixing bowl, beat eggs and add grated potato, onion and rest of ingredients. Add more matzo meal or flour if mixture seems too wet

Form 3-4" patties with your hands squeezing out any excess moisture

Heat 2-3 tbsp of oil on medium heat in sauté pan

Place patties down carefully in hot oil and let cook for 3-4 minutes on one side until you can see a little brown peeking out from underneath

Carefully flip latkes away from your face and cook for another 3-4 minutes

Remove latkes from pan and place on a paper towel-lined plate to remove excess oil. Keep warm in oven on lowest setting until all latkes are cooked

Serve with apple sauce and Caroline's Latke Sauce garnished with chives or scallions

CAROLINE'S LATKE SAUCE

Mix ingredients and serve on top or on the side of the latkes

NOTES

You can freeze your latkes after you've cooked them. Place them in a single layer on a parchment-lined pan and freeze them in a zip-top bag. When ready to reheat, take them directly from freezer and place on cookie sheet in 350°F oven for 15-20 minutes. Turn them over once to prevent burning.

HANUKKAH

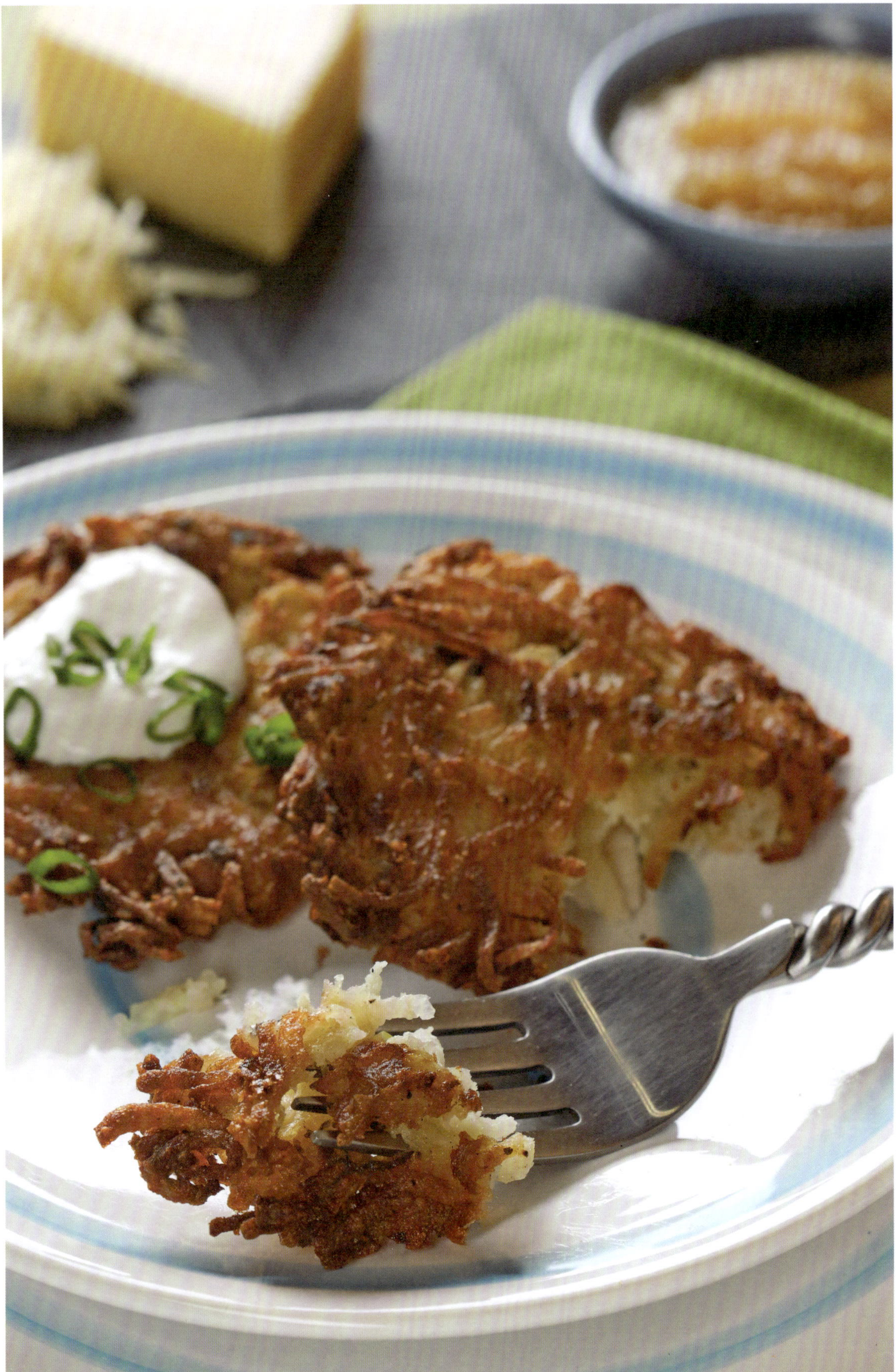

Potato and Cheddar Latkes with Horseradish Sour Cream

Many families and communities have their own latke variations. I like to make Potato and Cheese Latkes to celebrate the heroic story of Judith whose bravery and ingenuity saved the Jews. Judith served salty cheese and a lot of wine to the General Holofernes in order to get him drunk (Book of Judith 10:5). To commemorate Judith, we serve a lot of cheese dishes during Hanukkah. This latke variety is just plain delicious and the horseradish sour cream is the perfect companion.

Makes 10-12 Latkes

INGREDIENTS

LATKES

3 russet potatoes, peeled & grated

½ onion, peeled & grated

2 eggs

½ cup matzo meal or all-purpose flour

1 cup grated cheddar cheese

1 tsp salt

pepper to taste

apple sauce for garnish

vegetable oil for frying

HORSERADISH SOUR CREAM

1 16-oz container sour cream

2 tbsp grated white horseradish

INSTRUCTIONS

LATKES

Peel potatoes and onion and process with grating blade in food processor or grate by hand with box grater. Set aside

In large mixing bowl, beat eggs and add grated potato, onion and rest of ingredients. Add more matzo meal or flour if mixture seems too wet

Form 3-4" patties with your hands and squeeze out excess moisture

Heat 2-3 tbsp of oil on medium heat in sauté pan

Place patties down carefully in hot oil and let cook for 3-4 minutes on one side until you can see a little brown peeking out from underneath

Carefully flip latkes away from your face and cook for another 3-4 minutes

Remove latkes from pan and place on a paper towel-lined plate to remove excess oil. Keep warm in oven on lowest setting until all latkes are cooked

Serve with apple sauce and horseradish sour cream

HORSERADISH SOUR CREAM

Stir ingredients together and serve on top of latkes or on the side

NOTES

You can freeze your latkes after you've cooked them. Place them in a single layer on a parchment-lined pan and freeze them in a zip-top bag. When ready to reheat, take them directly from freezer and place on cookie sheet in 350°F oven for 15-20 minutes. Turn them over once to prevent burning.

Sweet Potato Latkes

In 2013, Thanksgiving and Hanukkah overlapped for the first time in many years. We called it Thanksgivukkah! As a nod to this amazing confluence, I made these Sweet Potato Latkes to marry the spirit of these two family and feast holidays.

Makes 10-12 Latkes

INGREDIENTS

2 large sweet potatoes, peeled & grated

3 eggs lightly beaten

½ onion, peeled & grated

½ cup matzo meal or all-purpose flour

½ tsp cinnamon

1 tsp salt

vegetable oil for frying

sour cream, apple sauce & cinnamon for garnish

INSTRUCTIONS

Peel sweet potatoes and process with grating blade in food processor or grate by hand with box grater. Set aside

In large mixing bowl, beat eggs and add grated sweet potato, onion and rest of ingredients. Add more matzo meal or flour if mixture seems too wet

Form 3-4" patties with your hands

Heat 2-3 tbsp of oil on medium heat in sauté pan

Place patties down carefully in hot oil and let cook for 3-4 minutes on one side until you can see a little brown peeking out from underneath

Carefully flip latkes away from your face and cook for another 3-4 minutes

Remove latkes from pan and place on a paper towel lined plate to remove excess oil. Keep warm in oven on lowest setting until all latkes cooked

Serve with apple sauce and sour cream with a little cinnamon sprinkled on top

NOTES

You can freeze your latkes after you've cooked them. Place them in a single layer on a parchment-lined pan and freeze them in a zip-top bag. When ready to reheat, take them directly from freezer and place on cookie sheet in 350°F oven for 15-20 minutes. Turn them over once to prevent burning.

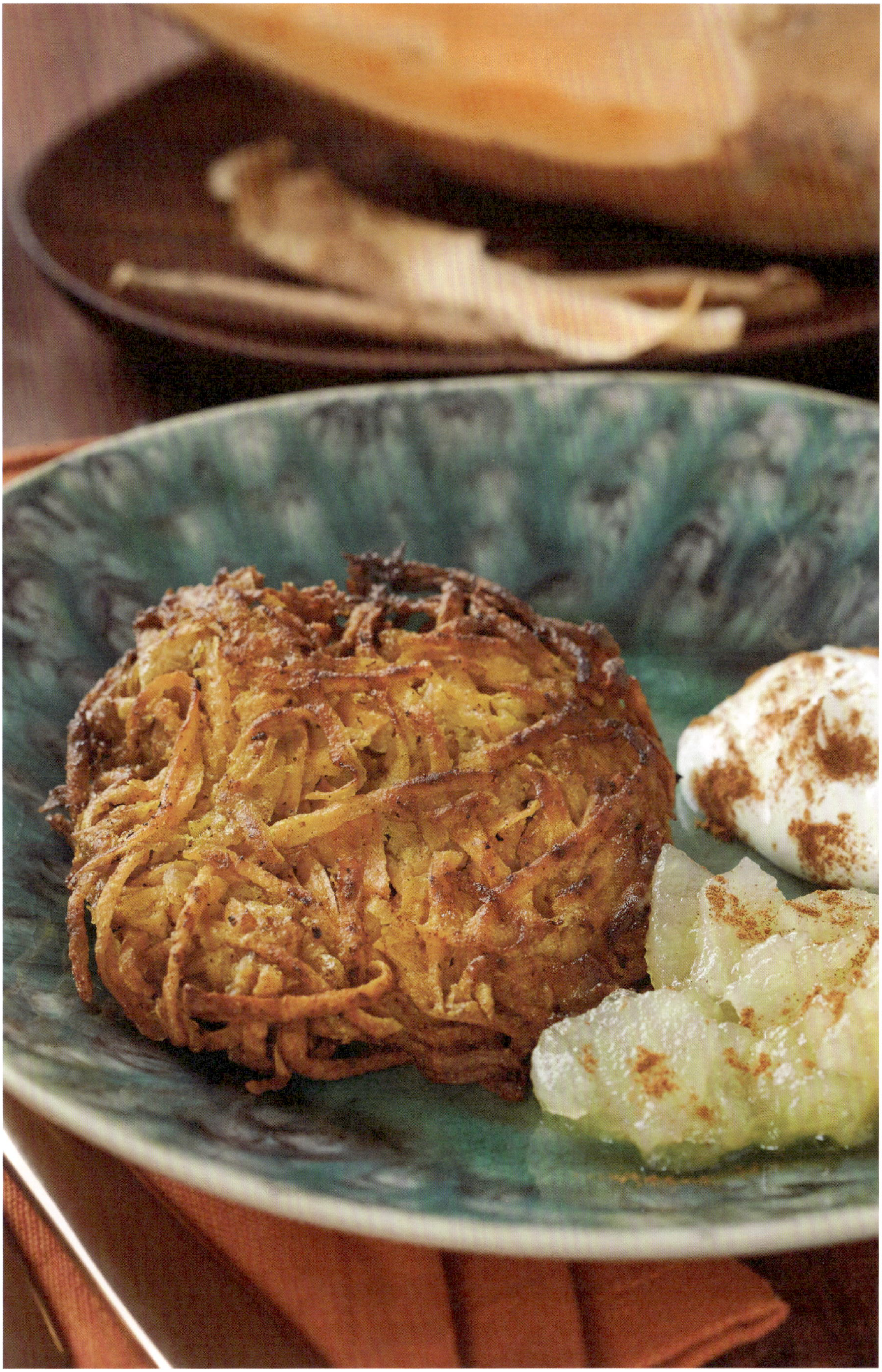

Gluten-Free Zucchini Latkes

GF

I decided to experiment with Zucchini Latkes when I wanted to explore a gluten-free option for friends. They turned out great. Fresh and light without losing their delectable crunchiness. It appears Zucchini Latkes are catching on. This summer, just after we'd tested our recipes and completed our photo shoot, we were delighted to see Zucchini Latkes appear on several restaurant menus.

Makes 10-12 Latkes

INGREDIENTS

3 large zucchinis, grated

½ onion, peeled & grated

1 egg, lightly beaten

¼ cup finely grated Parmesan cheese

½ cup arrowroot flour

1 tbsp fresh thyme + extra for garnish

1 tsp salt

pepper to taste

vegetable or canola oil for frying

sour cream to serve on top

INSTRUCTIONS

Cut zucchinis in half and process with grating blade in food processor or grate by hand with box grater

Place grated zucchini in a towel and squeeze out excess water

Grate onion and set aside

In large mixing bowl, beat eggs and add grated zucchini, onion and rest of ingredients. Add more arrowroot flour if mixture seems too wet

Form 3-4" patties with your hands. These latkes are more delicate than standard potato latkes so handle them with care

Heat 2-3 tbsp of oil on medium heat in sauté pan

Place patties down carefully in hot oil and let cook for 3-4 minutes on one side until you can see a little brown peeking out from underneath

Carefully flip latkes away from your face and cook for another 3-4 minutes

Remove latkes from pan and place on a paper towel-lined plate to remove excess oil. Keep warm in oven on lowest setting until all latkes are cooked

Serve with sour cream and fresh thyme on top

NOTES

You can freeze your latkes after you've cooked them. Place them in a single layer on a parchment-lined pan and freeze them in a zip-top bag. When ready to reheat, take them directly from freezer and place on cookie sheet in 350°F oven for 15-20 minutes. Turn them over once to prevent burning.

HANUKKAH

Marzipan Stuffed Dates

This is a delicious vegan Hanukkah dessert and fun family cooking project for your kids to help with! Making marzipan (almond paste) is easy and everyone can take part in creating their own unique stuffed date by picking the nuts of their choice or dipping them in chocolate. Almonds are a sign of spring so it's also delightful for Passover or any fun family gathering. You can serve this vegan dessert for Passover Seder, Succot or any fun family gathering.

Makes about 2 dozen stuffed dates

INGREDIENTS

FOR MARZIPAN

2 cups almond flour (or blanch, grind and dry your own almonds)

1-½ cups confectioners sugar

2 tsp almond extract

1 tsp rose water

1 egg white

FOR STUFFED DATES

Marzipan (either make from scratch per above or buy)

24 Medjool dates, pits removed

24 almonds (you can use any kind of nuts you like or even dip in chocolate)

INSTRUCTIONS

MAKE THE MARZIPAN

Put the almond flour and confectioners sugar in the bowl of a food processor and pulse until combined

Add almond extract and rose water and pulse again to combine

Add the egg white and process until a thick dough is formed

Remove the marzipan from the food processor bowl and form it into a log. Wrap it up in plastic and refrigerate

STUFF THE DATES

With a small spoon, scoop a little of the marzipan into each date leaving room for an almond

Garnish each with almonds or chopped nuts of your choice

NOTES

You can make the marzipan weeks ahead and store in a log shape, wrapped in plastic, until you're ready to use it.

Food grade rose water can be purchased on Amazon or in specialty stores.

HANUKKAH

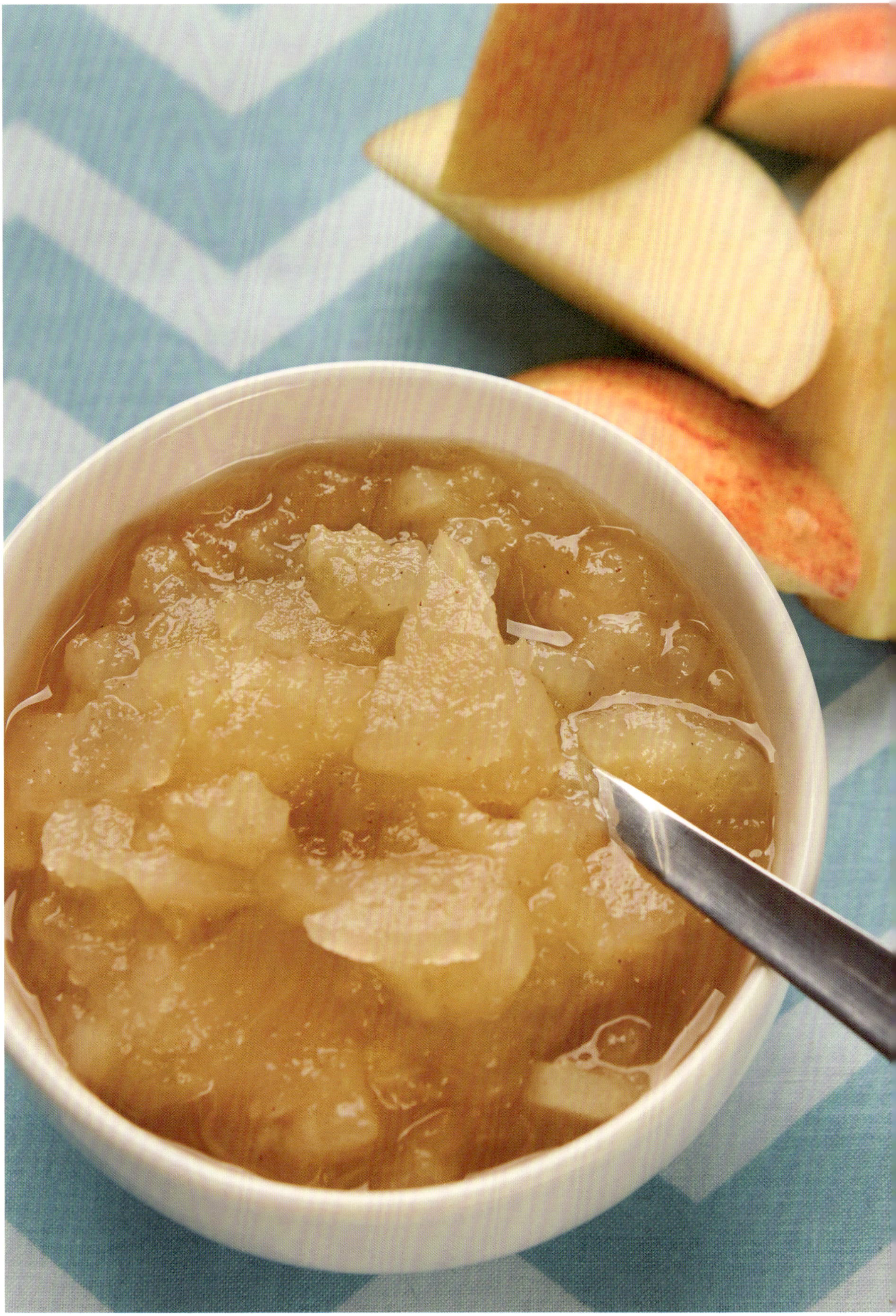

Caroline's Apple Sauce

V, GF

My daughter Caroline loves making homemade apple sauce. We keep it rustic instead of the traditionally puréed version because we like to keep the crunch of the apple. Originally we made this recipe because apple sauce is the classic, natural side dish for Hanukkah potato latkes. But this recipe was such a success in our house that we now make it for Thanksgiving and Rosh Hashanah as well!

Makes about 3 cups depending on size and water content of apples

INGREDIENTS

5 apples, peeled, cored & chopped

1 cinnamon stick

½ cup sugar

zest & juice of 1 lemon

½ cup water (or more as needed)

INSTRUCTIONS

Add all ingredients to saucepan

Bring to a boil then simmer until apples are soft (about 20-30 minutes depending on apples)

Remove cinnamon stick and serve immediately or refrigerate

Andy's Meat Sauce

GF

The wonderful array of ingredients in Andy's Meat Sauce including 3 kinds of meat, lots of fresh and dried herbs and red wine makes this sauce stand out and stand up to meatballs, lasagna or a simple plate of pasta. Andy's unique technique of blending the sauce base before cooking the sauce saves time and makes the whole process a bit easier. Sauce always tastes better the second day so if you have time, make it ahead.

Serves 10-12

INGREDIENTS

¼ cup olive oil

2 28-oz cans crushed tomatoes

1 can tomato paste

1 lb ground beef

1 lb ground veal

1 lb ground buffalo (or another pound ground beef or veal)

2 large onions, peeled & quartered

4 shallots, peeled & roughly chopped

8 cloves peeled garlic, 6 chopped (reserve 2 of the garlic cloves for sauce)

1 can anchovies

½ cup fresh basil

½ cup fresh oregano

1 tbsp dried basil

1 tbsp dried oregano

1 cup red wine

1 tsp salt

½ tsp pepper

INSTRUCTIONS

In a blender, purée crushed tomatoes, tomato paste, two cloves of garlic, fresh oregano, fresh basil and anchovies

Heat olive oil in large heavy-bottomed pot or dutch oven on medium-low heat. Add onions and shallots and sauté until they are translucent

Add chopped garlic (6 cloves) and sauté for an additional 1 minute. Stir constantly so you don't burn the garlic

Add the ground veal, beef and buffalo, salt and pepper and stir frequently until cooked through (5-8 minutes)

Add 1 cup of red wine. Bring to a boil and then simmer 10 minutes

Add dried basil and dried oregano to pot

Add the blended tomato sauce to the pot and let simmer for 1 hour, stirring frequently

Adjust salt and pepper seasoning as needed

Serve with our Classic Meatballs or over pasta

HANUKKAH

Za'atar Roast Chicken

A Jewish holiday table isn't truly complete without a beautiful roast chicken dish. We wanted a recipe for our Hanukkah chicken that would be meaningful for the holiday, so we looked to the Torah for inspiration. We came up with a fast and fun recipe that uses the traditional Middle Eastern spices of Za'atar and Hyssop, two spices with just enough biblical reference to make it special.

Za'atar is a popular and distinctive Israeli spice mix of dried thyme, toasted sesame seeds, ground sumac and salt. Hyssop is the term for wild thyme and was referenced in the Torah in the Story of Exodus (Exodus: 12:22-23). Combining the two together creates a chicken dish that is crisp on the outside and moist on the inside, and perfumes your home with a distinctly Israeli scent.

Za'atar Roast Chicken is also an excellent dish for Rosh Hashanah and Passover.

GF

Serves 4-6

INGREDIENTS

4-½ - 5 lb chicken

½ cup unsalted butter (1 stick), room temperature (to make kosher, use olive oil instead)

4 tbsp za'atar (blend of dried spices like thyme and oregano, sumac, sesame seeds and salt)

½ lemon, sliced

½ small onion, peeled & sliced

salt to taste (only use if there is no salt in your za'atar spice blend)

INSTRUCTIONS

Preheat oven to 375°F

Rinse and pat dry chicken

Combine za'atar with butter (or olive oil if you want to make dish kosher) and rub all over the chicken. Season with salt only if there is no salt in your za'atar spice blend

Stuff the chicken with lemon and onion slices

Place chicken in a small roasting pan or cast iron pan and bake at 375°F for 1 hour or until internal temperature reaches 160°F

Remove from oven and let rest for 10 minutes before slicing to retain juices

Slice and serve with roasted vegetables

HANUKKAH

Bubbie's Stuffed Cabbage

GF

A crowd-pleasing sweet, sour and savory marriage of ground meat, hearty cabbage, raisins and tomato. Stuffed Cabbage is perfect for Succot to celebrate the holiday and highlight cabbage as a fall harvest vegetable. We love to make these bundles with the help of the kids. They love to be put in charge of rolling up each cabbage leaf so that the meat mixture stays tucked safely inside. This is a great dish to make a day or two ahead so you can enjoy more time with your family.

Serves 12-20 depending on size of cabbage rolls

INGREDIENTS

1 large cabbage

FOR FILLING

2 cloves garlic, peeled & minced

1 onion, peeled & finely chopped

1 lb ground beef

1 egg

½ cup uncooked rice

½ cup raisins

1 tbsp cinnamon

2 tbsp fresh thyme, stems removed, roughly chopped

salt & pepper to taste

FOR TOMATO SAUCE

¼ cup olive oil

2 28-oz cans crushed tomatoes

½ onion, finely chopped

2 cloves garlic, minced

large handful of fresh thyme, stems removed, rough chopped

salt & pepper to taste

INSTRUCTIONS

PREPARE THE CABBAGE LEAVES

Boil a large pot of water big enough to lower a large cabbage into

Remove the core from the cabbage

Carefully place the cabbage into the boiling water and boil for 10-15 minutes. Once the cabbage leaves are tender and you can easily peel the outside layer away from the cabbage head, it is ready

Carefully remove the cabbage head from the boiling water and sit in a colander in your sink. Do not discard the boiling water yet. You may need it to cook some of the lower leaves of cabbage

Remove the cabbage layers and let cool on a cutting board or countertop surface

If inner leaves are still a little tough, put the rest of the cabbage head back into the boiling water

MAKE THE TOMATO SAUCE

In a large heavy-bottomed pan, heat the olive oil on medium heat

Add onion and turn heat to low. Cook onions until they are translucent

Add garlic. Sauté for a minute or so. Don't let the garlic burn

Add crushed tomatoes and let simmer for a couple minutes

Add thyme, salt and pepper and simmer for another 5 minutes or so

Remove from heat and let cool slightly

MAKE THE FILLING

Combine all filling ingredients in a large bowl and set aside

If making ahead, cover and refrigerate

ASSEMBLE THE CABBAGE ROLLS

First preheat the oven to 350°F so it will be ready when your rolls are complete

Lay a cabbage leaf down on a flat surface with core end facing you

Spoon about 3 tbsp of filling into your leaf in a log shape. You may need a little less or more depending on the size of your cabbage leaf

Fold the core side of the cabbage over the filling then fold in the sides over the filling

Roll the cabbage leaf away from you into a roll

Place in a large lasagna pan

Keep making your cabbage rolls and lining them up in your lasagna pan until you've used up all your filing. You should have 12-18 rolls depending on size of cabbage leaves, how much filling you use and how tightly you roll your cabbage

Pour your tomato sauce over the rolls

Cover your pan tightly with tin foil

Bake at 350°F for 1 hour and 30 minutes or until the rice is cooked to your liking

Chraime (Sephardic Fish Dish)

GF

Chraime is a delicious Sephardic recipe comprised of white fish prepared with a tangy and spicy tomato sauce highlighted with smoked paprika and fresh cilantro on top. Chraime is traditionally prepared by Sephardic Jews (such as Moroccan Jews and Israeli Jews of North African origin) for Friday night Shabbat dinner, Rosh Hashanah and Passover. In some ways, it is the Sephardic culinary answer to the traditional Ashkenazi Gefilte Fish.

Serves 4

INGREDIENTS

2 tbsp extra virgin olive oil

1 onion, peeled & finely chopped

1 lb skinless fish fillets (firm fish such as halibut, red snapper, cod)

2 large tomatoes, cored & diced

1 green chile or jalapeño, minced (more or less depending on how spicy you would like the dish)

1 roasted red pepper, diced (you can buy a jar of already roasted red peppers or char one in the broiler, remove the skin, veins and seeds and dice)

1 tbsp cumin

1 tsp smoked paprika

3 cloves garlic, peeled & minced

juice from ½ lemon

1-½ cups of water

handful of cilantro, roughly chopped

salt & pepper to taste

INSTRUCTIONS

Heat cumin and paprika in a hot heavy-bottomed pan for a minute until you can smell their aroma

Add olive oil to pan and turn heat to medium-low

Sauté onions until they are translucent

Add garlic and sauté for about a minute

Add tomatoes, hot pepper, roasted red pepper, lemon juice and water to pan. Bring to a boil and then turn down to simmer for 5 minutes

Add fish, cover pan and cook for 5-8 minutes or until fish is opaque

Add salt and pepper to taste

Turn off heat, add fresh cilantro and serve

NOTES

You can make the entire dish 1 or 2 days ahead except the fish and then reheat the cooked ingredients and add fresh fish.

HANUKKAH

Classic Meatballs

Great for special holidays/events, or whenever you're serving a crowd, these meatballs are full of flavor with two kinds of meat and a variety of herbs. Make them ahead and pop them out of the freezer whenever you're ready to cook and serve.

Makes 25-30 meatballs depending on size

INGREDIENTS

1 lb ground beef

1 lb ground veal

¼ cup breadcrumbs, fresh (keeps meatballs moister than dry breadcrumbs)

2 shallots, peeled & diced

1 tbsp dried oregano

1 tbsp dried basil

1 tbsp dried parsley

2 cloves garlic, peeled & chopped

½ cup Parmesan cheese (omit to make kosher)

2 eggs, slightly beaten

salt & pepper to taste

INSTRUCTIONS

Preheat oven to 350°F

Line a baking sheet with parchment paper

Combine all ingredients in a large bowl and form meatballs of desired shape

Take a small piece of the meatball mixture and cook on stovetop to ensure it is seasoned to your taste. Adjust if needed

Place meatballs on baking sheet and bake for 20-25 minutes (to test doneness with a meat thermometer, meatballs should be 160°F)

Enjoy as is or with Andy's Meat Sauce

NOTES

You can make the meatballs ahead and freeze them uncooked in a single layer on a baking sheet and then place them in a zip-top bag and back into freezer. When you want to cook them, remove from freezer and bake at 350°F for 25-30 minutes (no need to thaw them first).

HANUKKAH

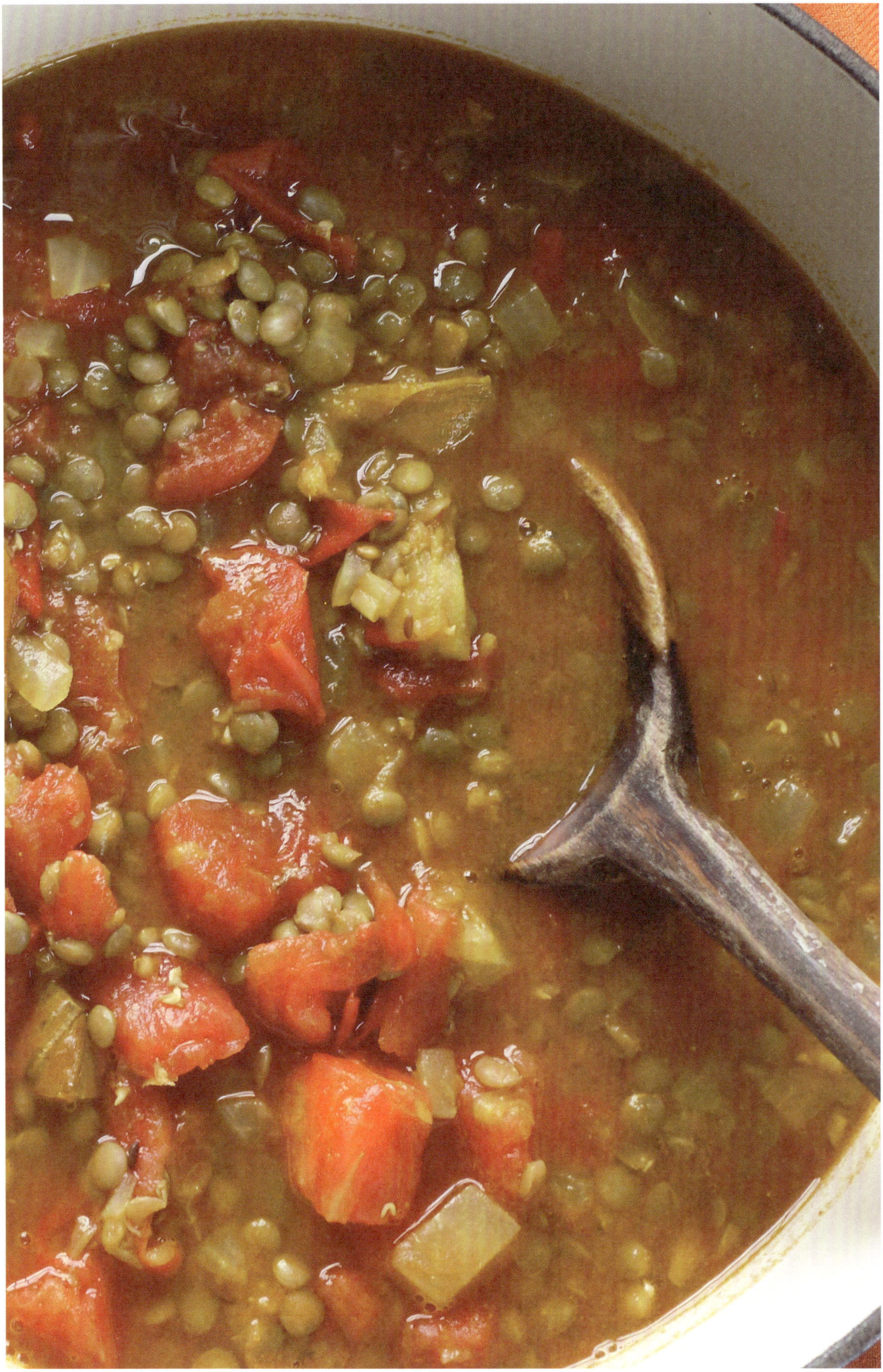

Lentil Curry over Cauliflower Mash

V, GF

This is a hearty vegan dish with lots of flavor and spice. We serve it over Cauliflower Mash (recipe included here as well) to soak up all those delicious curry juices.

Serves 8 people

INGREDIENTS

FOR THE CURRY

3 cups dried brown lentils

6 cups water

2 tbsp coconut oil

1 large onion, peeled & finely chopped

1 red chile, finely chopped (leave some seeds in for spice)

1 tbsp cumin

½ tsp garam masala

2 tsp ginger, peeled & minced

½ tsp cayenne pepper

2 tsp ground coriander

½ tsp turmeric

4 medium tomatoes, chopped

1 cup vegetable stock

2 tsp lemon juice

salt to taste

2 tbsp cilantro, chopped

FOR THE CAULIFLOWER MASH

4 whole cauliflowers

2 tbsp coconut oil

salt & pepper to taste

INSTRUCTIONS

MAKE THE LENTIL CURRY

Wash lentils with water and strain

Add lentils to a large pot and add 6 cups water

Bring to a boil then simmer for 10-15 minutes until lentils are soft but not mushy

Set aside

Heat a Dutch oven or heavy-bottom pan over medium heat and add coconut oil

Add onion and cook until translucent

Add ginger, chile and spices and cook until fragrant (1-2 minutes)

Add tomatoes, vegetable stock, lemon juice and salt and simmer for 5-10 minutes or until tomatoes have softened

Add cooked lentils and warm through for a minute or so

MAKE THE CAULIFLOWER MASH

Roughly chop the cauliflowers

Bring a large pot of water to a boil and add cauliflower

Cook about 10 minutes or until you can easily insert your knife in the cauliflower

Drain cauliflower and put in a large bowl

Add coconut oil, salt and pepper and mash with a hand masher or gently in a food processor

SERVE

Place a couple spoonfuls of Cauliflower Mash on the plate

Top with the Lentil Curry

Sufganiyot

Jelly Donuts

HANUKKAH

Sufganiyot (Jelly Donuts)

Every culinary culture has a doughy pastry fried in oil, a local version of the donut. Jews are no exception. Wherever Jews have lived throughout history, they've made a tradition of creating a special Hanukkah version of fried dough to celebrate the Miracle of Oil.

Ashkenazi Jews emigrating from Germany brought the Sufganiyot tradition to Israel in the 1930s. Who can resist these fluffy pillows of dough with your favorite jam filling inside. These always fly off the table. Make sure to get one before they're gone.

Makes 12-14

INGREDIENTS

3 cups all purpose flour + extra for dusting

1 tsp salt

1 packet active dry yeast (2-¼ tsp)

¾ cup warm milk

2 tbsp sugar + 2-3 more cups for coating the donuts

2 large eggs, lightly beaten

2 tbsp unsalted butter, melted & cooled

1 jar preserves/jelly of choice

vegetable oil for frying

cinnamon (optional for coating donuts)

EQUIPMENT

candy thermometer that you can clamp to the inside of your pot

INSTRUCTIONS

In a small bowl, combine 2 tbsp of warm milk (100-110°F) and 2 tbsp of sugar. Add the dry active yeast and let sit until foamy, about 5 minutes

In the bowl of a mixer, combine 3 cups flour and 1 tsp salt. Add yeast mix to the flour. Add the eggs and butter to the flour mixture. Mix the ingredients until they come together into a crumbly mix

Mix in the rest of the milk, 1 tbsp at a time until the dough sticks together in a ball

Turn the dough out onto a lightly floured surface and knead until the dough is smooth. (You can do this in a mixer fitted with a dough hook as well.) Form the dough into a ball and transfer it to a lightly oiled bowl, cover with a kitchen towel and let rise until doubled in size, about 2 hours

Punch down the risen dough. Turn out onto a lightly floured surface. With a lightly floured rolling pin, gradually roll out the dough to about ½" thick. When rolling dough, let it rest periodically to relax the dough and make it easier to roll out

Cut out 3-4" rounds with a lightly floured biscuit cutter or drinking glass. Re-roll the scraps to make more rounds

Place the donuts on lightly floured baking sheets that are lined with parchment paper, spacing them apart and cover lightly with a dry towel. Let rise in a warm spot until doubled in size, about 30 minutes

Heat a deep, heavy pot filled 3" high with vegetable oil to 350°F

Transfer the risen donuts to the pot and fry the donuts, a few at a time, until golden and puffed. About 1-2 minutes each side

Prepare a plate with 2-3 cups of mixed sugar and cinnamon

Lift the doughnuts from the oil using a slotted spoon and blot briefly on a paper towel-lined plate. While donuts are still hot, sprinkle with cinnamon-sugar (tongs are a good tool for holding the donuts). Set donuts aside

Fill a pastry bag (¼" round tip), squeeze bottle or zip-top bag with the corner cut off with jelly preserves. Insert the tip into the end of each donuts and pipe approximately 1-2 tbsp of preserves into them and serve

Scan for video

HANUKKAH

Loukoumades (Sephardic Greek Donuts)

Given the connection between the Jews and the Greeks in the Hanukkah story, in this recipe we celebrate the centuries-long culinary traditions of Greek Jews.

Loukoumades are a popular Greek fried-dough pastry. Greek Jews often call this classic Greek pastry Zvingous or Zvingoi and make them for Hanukkah. In Italy, the classic fried dough dish is Sfingi di San Giuseppe. In Spain and Mexico it is a Bimuelo.

Whatever they are called, and wherever they are made, these donuts are delightful treats made from deep fried dough coated with honey syrup. They differ from Sufganiyot in that the dough rises only once. The dough is a bit sticky but they are quicker to make. And you can infuse the honey syrup with your favorite flavorings. We used orange juice as well as rose water. Both delicious!

Makes 12-16

INGREDIENTS

DONUTS

1 packet active dry yeast (2-¼ tsp)

¾ cup water + 2 tbsp warm water to activate yeast

2-½ cups all-purpose flour

2 tsp sugar

1 egg, lightly beaten

pinch of salt

vegetable oil for frying

HONEY SYRUP

1 cup honey

1 cup water

1 tbsp rose water or orange juice

TOPPINGS

chopped pistachios

chopped walnuts

INSTRUCTIONS

MAKE THE HONEY SYRUP

Heat the honey and water until it is well combined

Take off heat and stir in the rose water or orange juice

Set aside

MAKE THE DOUGH

Pour contents of yeast packet into a bowl and mix in 2 tbsp warm water

Let yeast activate for about 10 minutes. Small bubbles should form

In a large bowl, combine the flour, sugar, egg and salt with a wooden spoon or whisk

Add the activated yeast

Slowly pour in the ¾ cup water until a sticky dough forms

Cover the bowl with plastic wrap and let rise in a warm place for an hour

FRY THE DONUTS

Heat a deep, heavy pot filled 3" high with vegetable oil to 350°F

Wet your hands and dip a large spoon in oil and spoon out some dough into your hands

It's tricky but try to form the dough into a round then carefully lower into the oil. If they come out in more of a fritter shape, don't worry. They will still taste delicious. You can also lighty oil a medium-sized cookie scoop (1-¾" diameter) and gently spoon the batter into the frying oil

Move the dough around in the oil with a slotted spoon until the donuts are lightly brown on all sides

Carefully remove from oil with slotted spoon and immediately lower into your Honey Syrup. Coat generously and place on serving platter or roll them in your favorite nuts. We love pistachios and walnuts

Eat immediately. They taste best warm

NOTES

Food grade rose water can be purchased on Amazon or in specialty stores.

Louisa's Kugel

In some families it's Noodle Pudding. In others it's Kugel. But in all families it is delicious. Our recipe is a classic with a twist that we think makes the dish extra special — apricot jam. Mildly decadent, easy-to-make, a creamy baked casserole of eggs, butter, noodles, luscious dairy, golden raisins and a good amount of sugar. Noodle pudding is the perfect make-ahead dish for a Hanukkah party. It really does taste better with the full-fat version, but it doesn't suffer when made with "light" dairy products.

Serves 12-14

INGREDIENTS

12-oz bag wide egg noodles

1 container cottage cheese (16 oz)

1 container sour cream (16 oz)

8 oz cream cheese, room temperature

4 eggs, lightly beaten

¾ cup sugar

1 tsp vanilla

pinch of salt

1 tbsp cinnamon + extra for dusting on top

2 cup raisins, golden or dark

1 cup slivered almonds

1 12-oz jar apricot jam

2 tbsp butter + extra for buttering the pan

INSTRUCTIONS

Preheat oven to 350°F

Coat 9"x13" (3-quart) baking dish with butter

Cook noodles according to package directions. Strain and set aside

Break eggs into a large bowl and whisk

Add dairy products to the bowl and mix

Gently fold in cooked noodles

Mix in vanilla, sugar and cinnamon

Fold in raisins

Pour mixture into baking dish

In a separate pan, heat apricot jam for 1 minute until the jam melts then pour jam over noodle mixture and spread with a pastry brush

Sprinkle slivered almonds on top, dust with cinnamon, dot with small pieces of butter, cover with tin foil and bake for 50 minutes

Uncover and bake for an additional 10 minutes so the top is slightly crunchy

Let cool slightly as it will be easier to serve

HANUKKAH

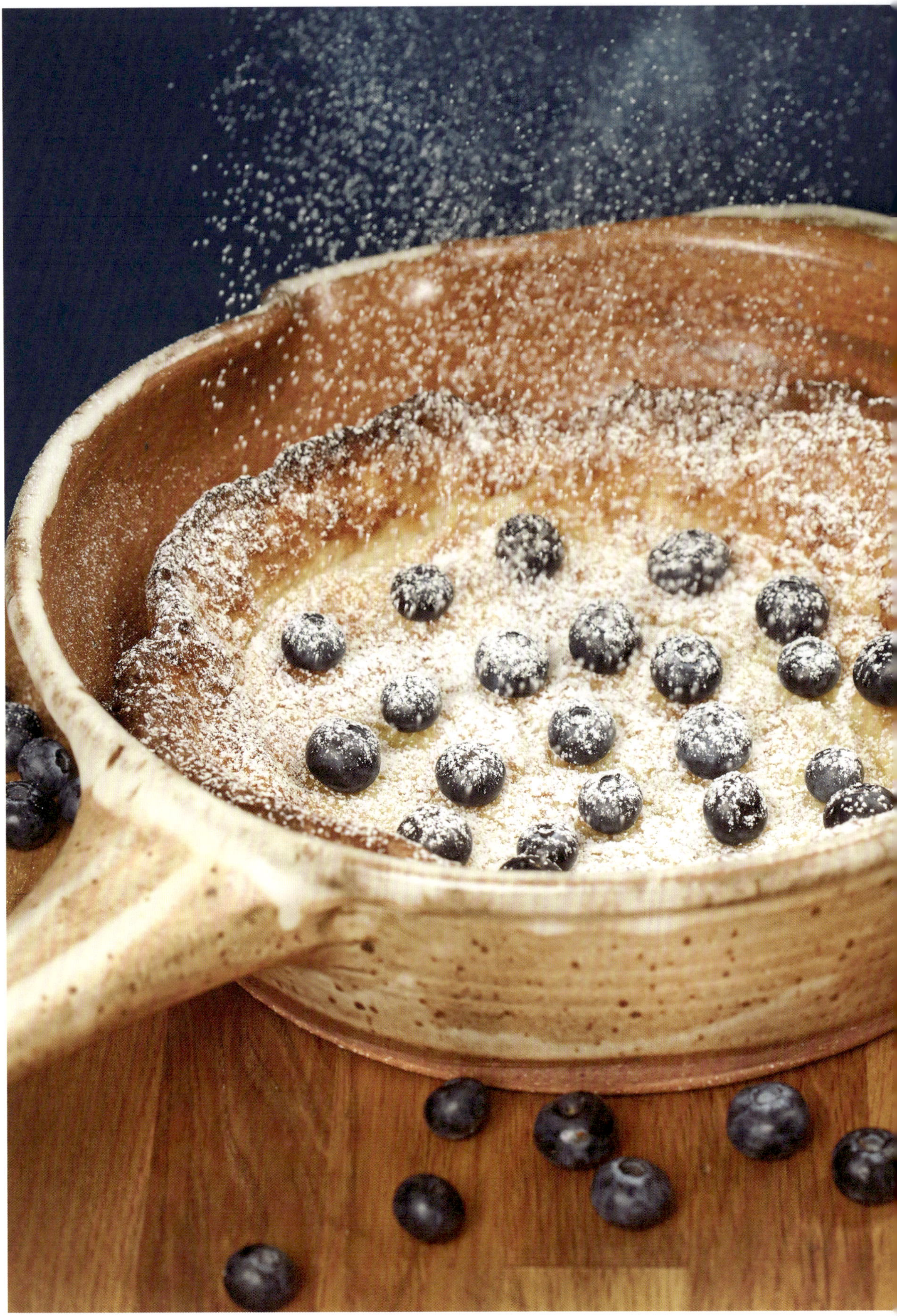

Nana's Puff Pancake

I've always loved my Mom's puffed pancake. (My kids call her Nana.) My mom truly inspired my love of cooking. This recipe was always a family favorite. It is sweet and tangy from the lemon and sugar combination. We loved eating it hot and also at room temperature. Either way, it is always a holiday treat!

Serves 4-6

INGREDIENTS

2 eggs

½ cup milk

½ cup all-purpose flour

½ tsp grated nutmeg

3 tbsp butter

juice & zest of 1 lemon

confectioners sugar for dusting on top

fresh blueberries for garnish

INSTRUCTIONS

Preheat oven to 425°F

Beat eggs lightly in bowl. Add milk, flour, lemon juice and zest and nutmeg and beat until blended

Melt butter in a 10" or 12" skillet over medium heat until butter froths

Pour in batter and remove pan from stove with pot holder and place in middle rack of oven

Bake for 15-20 minutes or until pancake has puffed up and browned

Remove from oven and let cool slightly so when you sift confectioners sugar on top it doesn't melt

Slice into wedges and garnish with blueberries and more confectioners sugar

HANUKKAH

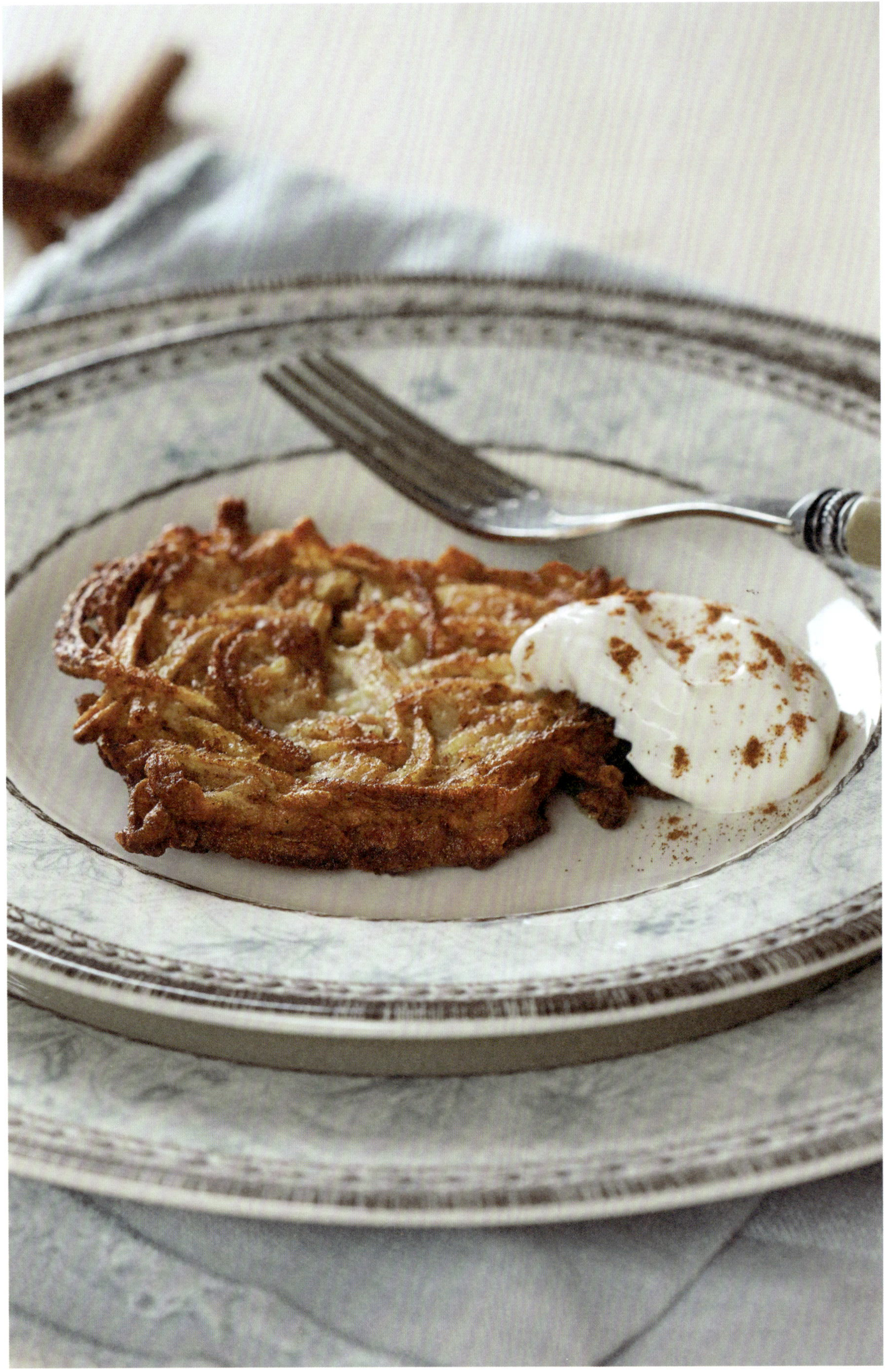

Apple-Cinnamon Dessert Latkes

We were inspired to make this apple latke variation in the fall when apples are fresh and abundant in New England. It's a delicious sweet latke option which pairs well with other Hanukkah desserts. Apple Latkes are also a wonderful addition to your Rosh Hashanah menu as they celebrate both the apples and the sweetness of the traditional Jewish New Year meal.

Makes 10-12 small dessert latkes

INGREDIENTS

5 apples, peeled, cored & grated or spiral cut

2 eggs, lightly beaten

½ cup all-purpose flour

2 tbsp arrowroot flour (helps absorb some of the moisture from apples)

1 tbsp sugar

1 tbsp cinnamon

vegetable or canola oil for frying

confectioners sugar for dusting

sour cream and apple sauce for serving on top

INSTRUCTIONS

Peel and core apples. Process in food processor with grating blade, grate by hand with box grater or make thin spirals with a spiralizer

In large mixing bowl, beat eggs and add all-purpose flour, arrowroot flour, sugar and cinnamon. Add more arrowroot flour if mixture seems too wet. Stir in grated apples

Form 3" patties with your hands, squeezing out extra moisture

Heat 2-3 tbsp of oil on medium heat in sauté pan

Place patties down directly from your spatula carefully in hot oil and let cook for 3-4 minutes on one side until you can see a little brown peeking out from underneath. It might seem like they are not going to hold together but they will

You may need to just nudge them with your spatula a little

Carefully flip latkes away from your face and cook for another 3-4 minutes

Remove latkes from pan and place on a paper towel-lined plate to remove excess oil. Keep warm in oven on lowest setting until all latkes are cooked

Serve with sour cream and apple sauce. Sprinkle confectioners sugar on top

NOTES

You can freeze your latkes after you've cooked them. Place them in a single layer on a parchment-lined pan and freeze them in a zip-top bag. When ready to reheat, take them directly from freezer and place on cookie sheet in 350°F oven for 15-20 minutes. Turn them over once to prevent burning.

Gelt (Chocolate Coins)

Gelt are a Hanukkah staple. Delicious to eat and a must for a game of Dreidel. So easy to make at home. It's a fun project so get the whole family involved in making and wrapping the chocolate.

INGREDIENTS

bag of chocolate chips or chunked chocolate

EQUIPMENT

double boiler

whisk

squeeze bottle

funnel

coin mold

gold & silver wrappers

INSTRUCTIONS

Melt chocolate in double boiler

Let cool slightly then pour in a squeeze bottle using a funnel to guide the chocolate into the bottle

Squeeze chocolate into the coin molds and put molds in freezer for 30 minutes minimum

Wrap coins in wrappers and refrigerate until Hanukkah

HANUKKAH

Vegan Chocolate Pudding

V, GF

Chocolate pudding with all the health benefits and none of the guilt? Yes please! Almost everyone likes a little something sweet now and then, and this recipe is perfect for those times. You also get the added benefit of antioxidants, healthy fats and gut-healthy green plantains. So dig in!

Serves about 8-10 half-cup servings

INGREDIENTS

4 tbsp raw cacao powder

1 cup coconut milk, refrigerated (spoon as much of the thick part into the blender as possible)

2 tbsp almond butter

2 green plantains (or 1 frozen banana)

pinch of monk fruit sweetener (or 6 pitted dates for added sweetness)

⅛ tsp ground cloves

1 cup of ice

handful of fresh mint and extra for garnish

INSTRUCTIONS

Put everything in a high-powered blender and purée. Should be a soft serve like consistency

Serve immediately in a small bowl with a sprig of mint

HANUKKAH

What is the Story of Hanukkah?

Many of us are more familiar with the symbols of the Hanukkah holiday — the Menorah, the dreidel, the latkes — than the story behind the holiday itself. Here's a little refresher course.

Hanukkah tells the story of Judah the Maccabee leading a small Jewish army in a revolt against Antiochus and his mighty Syrian Greek forces in the year BCE 164. At that time, the Greek Empire spread over a huge territory in the Middle East, including what is now Syria and the land of Israel. The Syrian Greeks ruled over the land of Israel and did not allow the Jews to practice their religion freely.

Mattathias, the High Priest of the Hasmoneans, led the initial revolt against the Syrian Greeks and appointed his son Judah the Maccabee ("The Hammer") as the leader. The Maccabees were greatly outnumbered by the Greeks, who had a vastly superior number of soldiers and fought on top of warrior elephants. Judah bravely led his small army in battle and through his skill defeated the Greeks.

According to legend, because the Greeks forbade religious study, the Jews studied Torah in secret and occupied the children by playing the dreidel (spinning top) so they would keep watch and warn the adults when the Greek soldiers were coming.

After the Maccabees triumphed over the Greek army, one of the first tasks was to clean and reorder the holy Temple, which had been defiled and ruined by the Greeks. According to the Talmud, when the Maccabees prepared to light the Menorah (candelabrum) which traditionally served as an eternal light in the Temple, they could find but one small jug of oil — a supply that was enough for only a single day. They searched and searched but couldn't find a source for more oil. Still, the Maccabees lit the Menorah and miraculously the oil lasted for eight days.

There are two major themes in the story of Hanukkah. Some rabbis emphasize the celebration of the Miracle of the Oil and how, according to the Talmud, because of the faith of the community, the oil lasted for 8 days when there was only one day's worth of oil.

Other sages, hewing closer to the Book of Maccabees, highlight the great military victory by the underdogs, the Maccabees, over the large, well-equipped Syrian Greek Army.

We find that both aspects of the Hanukkah story resonate. The Miracle of the Oil symbolizes God's care for the Jewish people, and the Jewish faith in God. Our pride in the Maccabee's victory complements this theme by reminding us of the need for bold human action in the face of challenge. We celebrate faith in God that allowed one day's oil to burn for eight, and we honor the heroic actions of the brave men and women who rescued their fellow Jews during the Maccabean Revolt and returned home to purify the Temple.

We continue to celebrate the Hanukkah story by lighting the Menorah each night of the eight-day celebration, eating foods like latkes and donuts that are cooked in oil and playing *Dreidel* and sharing Hanukkah *gelt* (coins) to remind us of the bravery of the heroic Maccabees.

HANUKKAH

Hanukkah Discussion Questions

1. Hanukkah is a holiday of rededication, a festival celebrating the re-establishment of the Holy Temple in Jerusalem by the Maccabees.

    Is there something in your life that you want to improve or to which you want to rededicate yourself this season?

2. Hanukkah celebrates the miracle of a small jug of oil lasting for 8 days.

    As you light your Menorah, ask this question: What "miraculous" events, large or small, do you wish to celebrate this year?

3. Hanukkah celebrates the victory of the underdogs, Judah the Maccabee and his band of rebels, over the great Syrian Greek army.

    What is an example of an underdog victory that makes you proud?

4. Judith was a heroine whose bravery and ingenuity helped save the Jewish people. The book of Judith (Yehudit in Hebrew), records that Holofernes, a Greek general, had surrounded the village of Bethulia as part of his campaign to conquer Judea. The fighting was intense and the situation became desperate. But Judith, a pious widow, told leaders she had a plan to save the city.

    Judith went to the Greek camp pretending to surrender. She met Holofernes, who was taken by her beauty. Judith agreed to go to his tent with him, where she plied him with cheese and wine.

    When Holofernes fell into a drunken sleep, Judith beheaded him and escaped. When Holofernes' soldiers found his beheaded corpse, they were overcome with fear. The Jews, on the other hand, were emboldened, and launched a surprise counterattack. The Syrian Greeks were defeated and the town was saved.

Who are some female heroes in your life? What great women leaders do you admire? Why?

5. Hanukkah has become a major gift-giving holiday. Sometimes, we focus too much attention on giving and receiving lavish gifts.

   Can you think of a way to share this holiday that might make a real difference to the lives of your family, friends, neighbors or even to strangers?

6. As we light the Menorah and recall the Miracle of the Oil (lasting for 8 days even though there was only enough oil to last 1 day), we have an opportunity to think carefully about the precious and limited natural resources of our planet.

   What is one practical action you can take to help preserve or re-new the great "temple" that is our planet by making the most of limited resources?

7. The dreidel and the Menorah are both important Hanukkah traditions. While our ancestors played the dreidel in order to protect their hidden study of Torah, we are instructed to play openly and display the Menorah for all to see.

   What is something you are proud of in your life? With whom do you share it? How do you share it?

8. On this final night of Hanukkah, the light of our Menorahs burn brightly with all of the candles aglow. According to tradition, we are not supposed to use the light of the Menorah for reading, studying or work. We are supposed to simply enjoy its wondrous light.

   What would you like to think about or discuss as you enjoy the beautiful light of the Menorah with your loved ones?

Shabbat

APPETIZERS
Potato-Leek Bourekas
Spinach and Feta Bourekas
Lebanese 7-Spice Kibbeh
Israeli Salad with Za'atar Dressing
Chopped Liver (Gehakteh Leber)

BREAD
Challah
Homemade Pita

DIPS & SAUCES
Tahini Sauce
Fig and Olive Tapenade

Shabbat is the celebration of sacred time, a weekly opportunity to rest and reflect. Shabbat means "to stop" and helps each of us pause and express gratitude for our blessings. It takes place just before sundown each Friday through the completion of nightfall on Saturday. No cooking is permitted during this time so all dishes must be prepared ahead or involve minimal warming.

Cholent is a signature dish of Shabbat. It's a delicious stew that can be slow cooked the day before and kept on low heat starting before and continuing through Shabbat. All of our Shabbat recipes are "make ahead" which is necessary but also perfect for everyday entertaining so you can spend less time in the kitchen and more time with your guests.

ENTREES
Slow Cooker Short Rib Cholent
Samkeh Harra (Fish with Spicy Sauce)
Falafel Wraps with Coconut Yogurt Sauce
Stuffed Portobello Mushrooms

DESSERTS
Chocolate Challah Bread Pudding
Etrog-Tahini Cookies
Apple-Cinnamon Parfaits

BEVERAGE
Mint and Rose Water Lemonade

V = Vegan

GF = Gluten Free

SHABBAT

Potato-Leek Bourekas

Imagine the most delicious mashed potatoes you've ever eaten wrapped in crunchy, flaky dough. That's what you can look forward to when you enjoy this tasty Turkish snack. Potatoes and leeks are a classic combination in soup and we thought they'd succeed in bourekas as well which they certainly do! Bourekas are the perfect part of your Succot celebration or a highlight of your Shabbat meal. For another delicious filling, try our Spinach & Feta Bourekas.

SHABBAT

Potato-Leek Bourekas

Makes 18 bourekas

INGREDIENTS

1 potato (about 10-12 oz), peeled & roughly chopped

2 tbsp butter (or olive oil) + extra if needed to smooth out potato mixture

1 leek, finely chopped (white part only), about ½ cup

1 tsp paprika

1 tsp cumin

pinch of cinnamon

½ tsp salt

1 clove garlic, peeled & minced

2 tsp fresh rosemary, very finely chopped (optional)

1 pound puff pastry sheets

flour for rolling out puff pastry (or roll pastry between parchment or plastic wrap sheets)

1 egg, beaten with 1 tsp water

2 tbsp sesame seeds (mix of black and white makes a nice presentation)

INSTRUCTIONS

MAKE THE FILLING

Place potato in a pot. Cover with water and add 1 tsp of salt

Bring to a boil, lower heat and simmer on medium-low for about 15-20 minutes or until you can easily insert a knife into the potato

Strain potato and roughly chop. Set aside

Heat a skillet on medium heat and add butter to pan

Add leeks, spices and salt and sauté until leeks are soft and translucent (about 3-5 minutes)

Add garlic and fresh rosemary to pan and sauté for about 1 minute

Add chopped potato to pan and toss with other ingredients for 1-2 minutes

Mash the potato mixture by hand or pulse in a food processor until combined (doesn't have to be perfectly smooth). Add a little extra butter or olive oil if mixture seems too dry

Taste and adjust seasoning if needed

You can store the filling for 2-3 days covered in the refrigerator

ROLL, FILL, FOLD & BAKE

Preheat oven to 350°F

Remove 1 pastry sheet at a time from freezer and let thaw about 5 minutes on your countertop. Just until you can gently unfold the pastry sheet

Sprinkle flour on countertop and roll out puff pastry into approximately a 10"x10" square. Alternatively, you can avoid the flour and keep your counter clean by rolling out the pastry between sheets of parchment paper or plastic wrap

Using a pizza wheel or bench scraper, cut the pastry into 9 squares

Place a tablespoon of the potato filling a little off center toward one corner of each square. With your fingertip or a brush, apply a little water around the edges of the square. Fold over the pastry into a triangle and seal the edges with your fingers or the tines of a fork

Place each finished boureka on a parchment-lined baking sheet. Repeat for all 9 squares and place in refrigerator or freezer while you roll out the second sheet of puff pastry and make your second batch of bourekas. If you have a little leftover filling, enjoy it as a side dish with dinner

At this point, you can either bake your bourekas or freeze them in a single layer then store them in a container or freezer bag

To bake, brush each boureka with egg wash and sprinkle with sesame seeds

Place your bourekas on a lined baking sheet and bake at 350°F for 20-25 minutes or until the bourekas have puffed up and lightly browned. Best enjoyed warm out of the oven

NOTES

If you freeze the bourekas, when you bake them, remember to brush them with an egg wash and top with sesame seeds. Preheat the oven to 350°F and bake for about 30-35 minutes or until bourekas have puffed up and are lightly browned.

Spinach and Feta Bourekas

Make them fresh or fill your freezer with dozens of these tasty Turkish snacks. Flaky pastry layers on the outside house a creamy spinach and feta mixture inside. Perfect for your Succot celebration or a highlight of your Shabbat meal. For another delicious flavor, try our Potato Leek Bourekas.

Makes 18 bourekas

INGREDIENTS

4-½ cups spinach

1 tbsp olive oil

½ small onion, peeled & finely chopped (about ¼ cup)

1 clove garlic, peeled & minced

2 tsp fresh thyme, finely chopped (optional)

1 tsp paprika + extra for sprinkling on top of bourekas before baking

1 tsp cumin

⅓ cup feta cheese

½ tsp salt, divided

1 tbsp pine nuts, roughly chopped

1 lb puff pastry sheets

flour for rolling out puff pastry (or roll pastry between parchment or plastic wrap sheets)

1 egg, beaten with 1 tsp water

2 tbsp sesame seeds (mix of black and white makes a nice presentation)

INSTRUCTIONS

MAKE THE FILLING

Heat a skillet on medium heat and add olive oil

Add chopped onion to pan and sauté until soft and translucent

Add garlic, spices, fresh thyme and ¼ tsp salt to pan and sauté for about a minute

Add spinach and sauté until spinach has completed wilted

Remove and strain excess liquid from the cooked spinach mixture. Squeeze out remaining liquid with hands or wrap in a towel and squeeze out

Finely chop the cooked spinach mixture and put in a medium size bowl

Add ¼ tsp salt and crumbled feta cheese and combine all ingredients together

Taste and adjust seasoning if needed

You can store the filling for 2-3 days covered in the refrigerator

ROLL, FILL, FOLD & BAKE

Preheat oven to 350°F

Remove 1 pastry sheet at a time from freezer and let thaw about 5 minutes on your countertop. Just until you can gently unfold the pastry sheet

Sprinkle flour on countertop and roll out puff pastry into approximately a 10"x10" square. Alternatively, you can avoid the flour and keep your counter clean by rolling out the pastry between sheets of parchment paper or plastic wrap

Using a pizza wheel, bench scraper or round-edged knife, cut the pastry into 9 squares

Place a tablespoon of the spinach and feta filling

a little off center toward one corner of each square. With your fingertip or a brush, apply a little water around the edges of the square. Fold over the pastry into a triangle and seal the edges with your fingers or the tines of a fork

Place each finished boureka on a parchment-lined baking sheet. Repeat for all 9 squares and place in refrigerator or freezer while you roll out the second sheet of puff pastry and make your second batch of bourekas. If you have a little leftover filling, enjoy it as a side dish with dinner

At this point, you can either bake your bourekas or freeze them in a single layer then store them in a container or freezer bag

To bake, brush each boureka with egg wash and sprinkle with sesame seeds and a little paprika

Place your bourekas on a lined baking sheet and bake at 350°F for 20-25 minutes or until the bourekas have puffed up and lightly browned. Best enjoyed warm out of the oven

NOTES

You can freeze Bourekas and pop them directly in the oven when you want to serve them. If you freeze the bourekas, when you bake them, remember to brush them with an egg wash and top with sesame seeds. Preheat the oven to 350°F and bake for about 30-35 minutes or until bourekas have puffed up and are lightly browned.

Lebanese 7-Spice Kibbeh

Crunchy on the outside, meaty on the inside, Lebanese 7-Spice Kibbeh are an addictive snack as is or with a nice dip in Tahini Sauce and some Tabbouleh and Israeli Salad on the side. My family and I just love Lebanese food. This is the perfect dish for your Shabbat dinner or Succot celebration.

Makes 24

INGREDIENTS

FOR THE "SHELL"

- 1-½ lbs ground beef
- 1-½ cups fine bulgur, rinsed
- 1 large onion, peeled & finely chopped
- 2 tbsp lemon juice
- 1 tbsp olive oil
- 2 tsp salt
- 1 tbsp Lebanese 7-Spice* (you can also use a combination of equal parts cumin and smoked paprika)

FOR THE FILLING

- 1 tbsp extra virgin olive oil
- ½ lb ground beef
- ½ small onion, finely chopped
- 1 tbsp lemon juice
- 1 tbsp pine nuts, toasted and roughly chopped
- 1 tsp Lebanese 7-Spice* (you can also use a combination of equal parts cumin and smoked paprika)
- 1 tsp salt

FOR FRYING

vegetable oil or coconut oil

*Lebanese 7-Spice: There are variations on what the 7 spices are but the blend we used contains: allspice, pepper, cinnamon, cloves, nutmeg, fenugreek and ginger

INSTRUCTIONS

MAKE "SHELL"

Soak bulgur for 30 minutes in cold water then strain

Put bulgur, 2 tsp lemon juice, 1-½ lb ground beef, onion, 2 tsp salt and seasoning in the bowl of a food processor until ingredients are fully combined and form into a ball

Set aside or refrigerate until ready to fill

MAKE FILLING

Heat sauté pan over medium heat and add extra virgin olive oil

Add onions and sauté until soft and translucent

Add ½ lb ground beef, salt and spices and sauté until beef is cooked through

Take off heat and stir in lemon juice and pine nuts

Cook a tbsp size of the filling in a sauté pan to taste and adjust seasoning if needed

FORM THE KIBBEH

Take about 2 tbsp of "shell" mixture and form it into a football shape

Make a hole with your thumb, stuff some filling inside and close up the football shape. Repeat until you have used all the mixture. You should have about 2 dozen kibbeh

You can cook them immediately but it helps to chill them in the refrigerator for about an hour first to ensure they hold up well when frying

FRY THE KIBBEH

Heat about 2" of oil in a heavy-bottomed pot to 350°F. Be sure to have a pan at least 5-6" high so the oil doesn't splash out of the pan

Carefully lower 2-3 kibbeh at a time in the oil and cook for 3-4 minutes, turning occasionally for even frying. They should be a nice deep brown color

When ready, carefully remove from oil with slotted spoon and place on a paper towel to remove some of the oil. Best enjoyed fresh out of the fryer!

NOTES

You can freeze your kibbeh before frying on a flat surface then stack in a container or freezer bag. When you're ready to cook them, remove from freezer and fry without thawing in 350°F oil for about 4-5 minutes.

Israeli Salad with Za'atar Dressing

V, GF

Light up your Shabbat table or your succah with a bright, fresh and healthy Israeli Salad. We have added za'atar to the recipe to add a little extra flavor. You can serve this as a simple appetizer or side dish but we also love to prepare little Pita pockets with a handful of salad, Kafta and Tahini Sauce. This is a perfect dish for your Shabbat luncheon or Succot celebration.

Serves 4-6

INGREDIENTS

FOR THE SALAD

4 tomatoes, deseeded, chopped & strained of excess liquid

3 Middle Eastern (also called Armenian or Persian) cucumbers or 1 English cucumber, chopped (leave peel on)

½ cup fresh parsley, chopped

½ cup fresh mint, chopped

½ red onion, peeled & finely chopped

FOR THE DRESSING

¼ cup olive oil

juice of 2 lemons

1 tsp za'atar

½ tsp salt

INSTRUCTIONS

Add chopped tomatoes, cucumbers, parsley and mint to a large bowl

Put lemon juice and za'atar in a separate bowl and whisk in olive oil

Add salt and adjust seasoning if necessary

Spoon a few teaspoons of dressing into the bowl at a time and toss

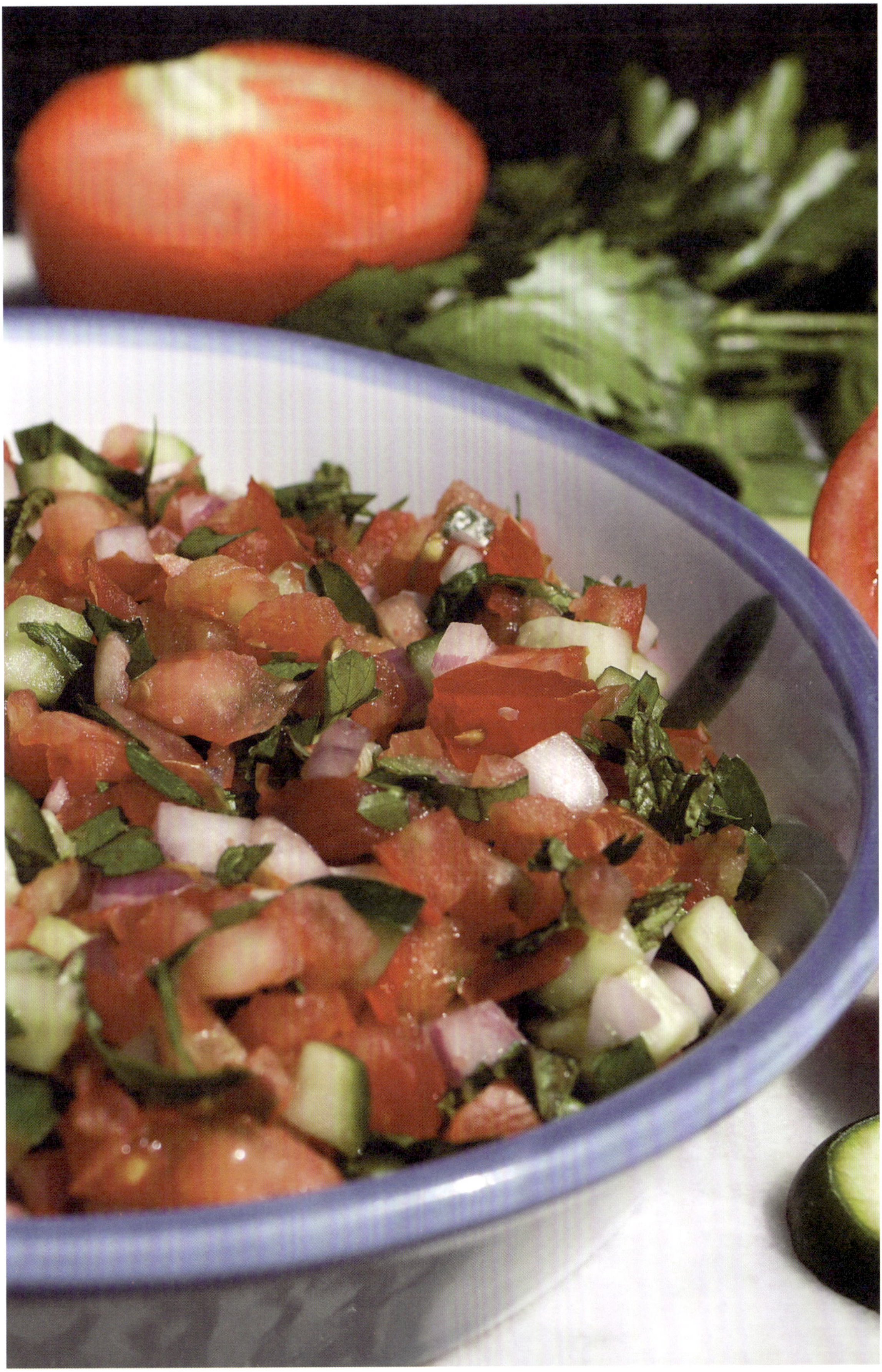

GF

Chopped Liver (Gehakteh Leber)

We love Chopped Liver. So earthy and rich, a single bite is a reminder of all the flavors of classic Jewish cooking. We developed this recipe because it is "fast and fun" to make and is so tasty. Our friends look forward to it each year.

My favorite part of the recipe is Lucy's Special Sauce. Lucy began to make this when she was 5 years old. She was so cute and proud, and I am still thrilled when she joins me to make this dish.

Makes 1 quart

INGREDIENTS

CHOPPED CHICKEN LIVER

- 1 lb chicken livers
- 8 garlic cloves, peeled (do not chop)
- 2 large onions, chopped
- 4 tbsp schmaltz (or olive oil)
- 4 hard boiled eggs, peeled and chopped
- 1 tsp salt + extra salt for rinsing livers
- ¼ tsp black pepper

LUCY'S SPECIAL SAUCE

- ½ cup ketchup
- 1 tbsp paprika
- ⅓ cup mayonnaise

INSTRUCTIONS

CHOPPED CHICKEN LIVER

Preheat broiler

Rinse chicken livers in salt water and pat dry

Toss livers and garlic with 1 tbsp of the schmaltz and broil them on a foil-lined pan for 10 minutes or until the livers are browned on the outside and cooked through on the inside (cut one open to check — should not be pink inside). Turn occasionally to ensure they don't burn

While the livers and garlic are cooking, sauté onions in the remaining 3 tbsp of schmaltz in a large skillet on medium heat until golden brown

When the livers and garlic are done, add them to the sauté pan, stir in with the onions and cook for another 3-4 minutes, stirring occasionally

Combine cooked liver, garlic and onions. Add hard boiled eggs, salt and pepper

Puree mixture until smooth or hand chop if you prefer

Serve chilled with Lucy's Special Sauce

LUCY'S SPECIAL SAUCE

Mix ketchup, paprika and mayonnaise in a bowl and serve with Chopped Chicken Liver and matzo crackers

NOTES

The Kosher technique to cook chicken liver, commonly known as kashering liver, is accomplished by soaking the liver in water, salting it and then rewashing it. Since chicken liver contains such a large concentration of blood, broiling is also necessary. Chicken livers can be broiled whole without cutting the surface.

SHABBAT

Challah

I first fell in love with the magic of challah when my uncle Rabbi Daniel Goldfarb made homemade Challah for my brother Laurence's Bar Mitzvah. My uncle flew from Israel for my Bar Mitzvah as well as for each of my brothers. He always baked the Challah for our Shabbat dinner. It really tasted so delicious and I fully appreciated the love with which he baked it.

We're so happy to bring our Challah recipe to all of you. There's nothing like the smell of fresh Challah bread baking in your oven. While making bread can seem daunting, we have created a step-by-step recipe and video to make it easier for you to master making and braiding a 4-strand Challah. Take your time and you'll soon be an expert!

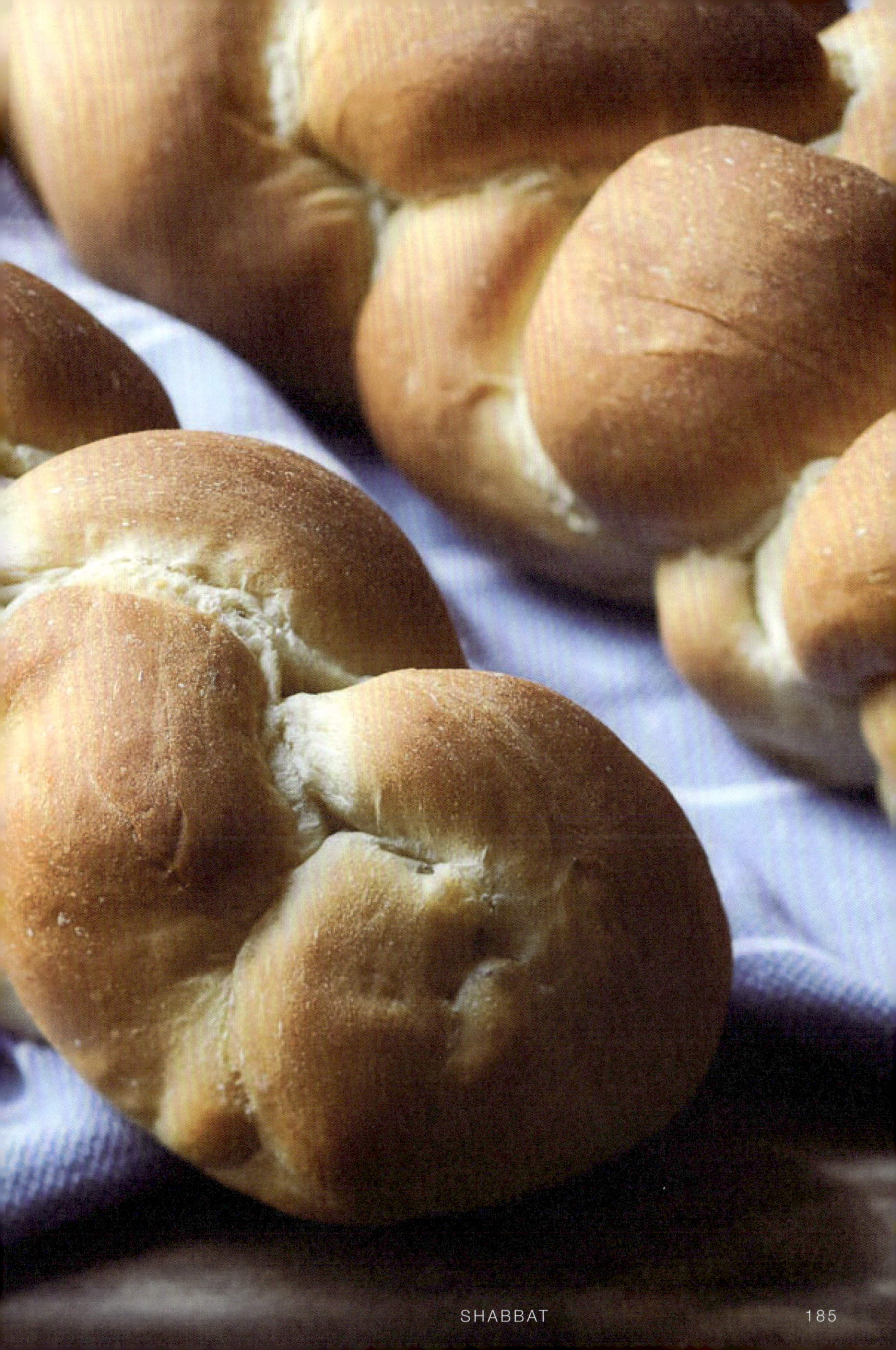

Challah

Makes 2 loaves

INGREDIENTS

1 cup warm water

1 tbsp + 1 tsp yeast

¼ cup honey

5 cups of all-purpose flour (plus extra for dusting work surface and kneading dough)

3 whole eggs

1 tbsp salt

¼ cup vegetable oil plus extra to oil the bowl for your dough

1 egg white (for glaze)

INSTRUCTIONS

MAKE THE DOUGH

In a mixing bowl combine the water, yeast and honey. Stir and let sit for a minute to activate the yeast

Mix eggs and flour in and stir until the ingredients start to come together (you can also mix using a dough hook attachment on your mixer)

Add salt and vegetable oil and continue to mix with a wooden spoon until dough forms a ball

Turn dough out onto lightly floured surface. Knead the dough, adding small amounts of flour if dough is too sticky, making ¼ turns for 6-8 minutes until the dough is smooth and not sticky (don't knead to the point the dough rips)

Place dough in an oiled bowl, cover, let rise in a warm area for 1 to 1-½ hours until dough doubles in size

BRAID THE CHALLAH (FOR 1 LOAF)

Note: You can practice this technique with ribbons or string first if you're a little nervous. It's easy once you get the hang of it.

Once the dough has risen, punch it down and divide in half to make your first loaf (Note: If not making the second loaf right away, put back in oiled bowl, cover and place in refrigerator)

Divide your dough into 4 equal pieces, about 4 oz. each

Roll strands into equal-length cylinders

Pinch strands together at one end

Take strand on far left, bring over two strands then weave the strand under the strand to your left

Take strand on far right, bring over two strands and weave the strand under the strand to your right. Repeat until whole loaf is braided

Tuck loose ends at end of braid underneath and pinch to keep in place

Place the loaf on a parchment-lined baking sheet, cover loosely with a kitchen towel, let rise in a warm area for ½ hour

BAKE THE CHALLAH

Preheat oven to 350°F

Brush egg white glaze on top of loaf (optional: sprinkle sesame seeds or poppy seeds on top)

Bake for 30-35 minutes, turning loaf once at 20 minutes to ensure bread bakes evenly

Loaf is done when golden brown

NOTES

We doubt you will have any leftover Challah in your house but if you do, use it to make delicious French toast or our Chocolate Challah Bread Pudding.

SHABBAT

Homemade Pita

You MADE the pita?! That's a question we often get when we bring homemade pita to the table. Don't tell anyone but it's really not that hard. Just takes time and patience while you wait for the rise. We find pita to be the perfect companion for our Kafta, Tabbouleh and Tahini Sauce — perhaps for your next Shabbat meal or Succot celebration.

Makes 12-16 pita rounds

INGREDIENTS

3-½ cups flour + extra for flouring work surface and working dough

2 tsp active dry yeast + a little warm water to activate the yeast

1 cup water

2 tsp salt

2 tbsp extra virgin olive oil

1 tbsp honey

INSTRUCTIONS

Mix yeast with a little warm water and set aside for 5 minutes

Add flour to a large bowl and mix in yeast mixture, honey and ½ cup water

Add salt and extra virgin olive oil

Add more water a little at a time until the dough comes together (it will be sticky)

On a floured surface, knead the dough for 10 minutes (you can also knead the dough in a stand mixer using the dough hook — 8 minutes). Add flour along the way to minimize the amount of dough that sticks to your fingers. The dough will still be slightly sticky

Place the dough in a bowl oiled with a little olive oil, cover with a towel and let sit in a warm, draft-free area for 1 hour or until the dough doubles in size

When dough has risen, punch it down, remove from the bowl, place on a floured service and divide into 4 equal pieces. Put 3 of the pieces aside and cover with a damp towel

Make a rectangular log out of the piece you have out and divide into 4 equal pieces. Take each piece and form it into a little round circle. Place on a floured baking sheet

Repeat for the remaining 15 pieces

NOTES

If you don't have room for all 16 pieces, you can place some of the dough back in the refrigerator, wrapped or covered (it will continue to rise so allow room).

Cover the rounds with a damp towel and let rise for 10 minutes.

Roll rounds out one at a time with a rolling pin on a lightly floured surface to 4-6" in diameter, keeping the others covered with a towel. (You can also just flatten the dough with the palm of your hand and gently stretch them into shape.) Place rolled out dough portions on a lightly floured cookie sheet. Depending on the size of your oven, you can probably fit 2-4 pitas on a cookie sheet at a time.

Cover the rolled out dough for another 5 minutes.

In the meantime, preheat your oven to 500°F.

Bake the pitas for 4 minutes on one side, flip and cook for another 1 minute on the other side. Remove from oven and move pitas immediately to a basket or bowl so they don't burn.

Continue to roll out dough and bake until you have as many pitas as you'd like.

Serve immediately or store covered securely with plastic wrap and serve within a couple of days. You can refrigerate the dough after the first rise. Just wrap loosely since the dough will continue to rise. When ready to bake, remove from the refrigerator and roll out per the instructions above — no need to let it sit out.

Scan for video

Tahini Sauce

V, GF

Tahini Sauce is a tasty addition to your Shabbat luncheon and Succot celebration. It is easy healthy, vegan and easy to make in advance. It's great as a dip with vegetables or a spread in a Pita sandwich with Kafta and Tabbouleh.

Makes about 2-¼ cups depending on desired consistency

INGREDIENTS

2 cups tahini

juice & zest of 2 lemons

1 tbsp olive oil

1 clove garlic, peeled & finely minced

salt & pepper to taste

water as needed

1 tsp smoked paprika (optional)

INSTRUCTIONS

Place all ingredients in a food processor and purée

If sauce is too thick, stream in water until the sauce is thinner and smooth

Fig and Olive Tapenade

V, GF

You've probably had olive tapenade before but we've added a little twist — dried black mission figs. The combination of sweet and savory flavors makes for a unique dip your guests will really enjoy. We like to serve it with fresh vegetables and/or crackers.

INGREDIENTS

¼ cup extra virgin olive oil

1 cup stemmed & quartered black figs (black Mission figs are ideal)

2 anchovy fillets

2 cups pitted black olives

3 tbsp lemon juice

4 tsp whole grain mustard

2 garlic cloves, peeled & minced

1 tbsp capers packed in salt (not brine) — rinsed and patted dry

2 tsp fresh thyme leaves, chopped (plus extra for garnish)

black pepper to taste

sea salt if necessary (taste tapenade before adding any salt)

INSTRUCTIONS

Pulse all ingredients in a food processor

Serve room temperature or chill

NOTES

You can make the Tapenade 3-4 days ahead and keep in the refrigerator.

SHABBAT

Slow Cooker Short Rib Cholent

Necessity is the mother of invention which accounts for Cholent, a dish you can create ahead of time so you can easily follow the Jewish law of not cooking on the Sabbath. Braised low and slow for 14+ hours, Cholent is the ultimate comfort food. Our version has tender brisket, beans and barley along with white potatoes, sweet potatoes and onions. A bouquet of fresh herbs adds another layer of flavor we think you'll find irresistible. We hope you will love our favorite Shabbat dish and share it with your loved ones.

Serves 6-8

INGREDIENTS

2 large sweet onions, peeled, roughly chopped & divided (1 roasted, 1 raw for slow cooker)

3 lbs short ribs, cut into 4" pieces

1 large sweet potato, peeled & roughly chopped

2 medium size potatoes, peeled & roughly chopped

2 large carrots, peeled & roughly chopped

1 bulb fennel, roughly chopped & divided (½ roasted, ½ raw in slow cooker)

1-½ cups dried beans (mixed or one type — recommend kidney, lima or heirloom beans), soaked overnight in filtered water

1 cup barley

1 tbsp cumin

1 tbsp salt + extra for seasoning the meat before roasting

1 tsp freshly ground pepper

herb bundle: 3-4 sprigs of rosemary and 6-8 sprigs of thyme, tied up in cheesecloth

water to cover ingredients in slow cooker

INSTRUCTIONS

ROAST MEAT AND VEGETABLES

Preheat oven to 450°F

Season your meat generously on both sides with salt and add to a large rectangular baking dish (glass or roasting pan)

Nestle in your chopped vegetables: 1 onion, 2 carrots and ½ bulb fennel

Roast for 20 minutes on one side, flip meat and toss vegetables. Roast for 10 more minutes

Remove meat and vegetables, put your pan over a burner and add 2 cups of water to deglaze the pan

Let the liquid reduce over medium heat for about 4-5 minutes then set aside

FILL SLOW COOKER

To your slow cooker, add beans and barley and raw chopped vegetables: 1 onion, ½ fennel bulb, 2 potatoes and 1 sweet potato

Add your roasted meat and vegetables

Add your herb bundle, cumin and salt

Add the reduced stock from your pan

Cover ingredients with water and set your slow cooker for 14-16 hours

If there's too much liquid for your liking, use a slotted spoon to plate your dish. Also, once you refrigerate the leftovers, the stew will thicken

NOTES

If you have leftovers, you can freeze them. Simply reheat straight from the freezer when you're ready to eat.

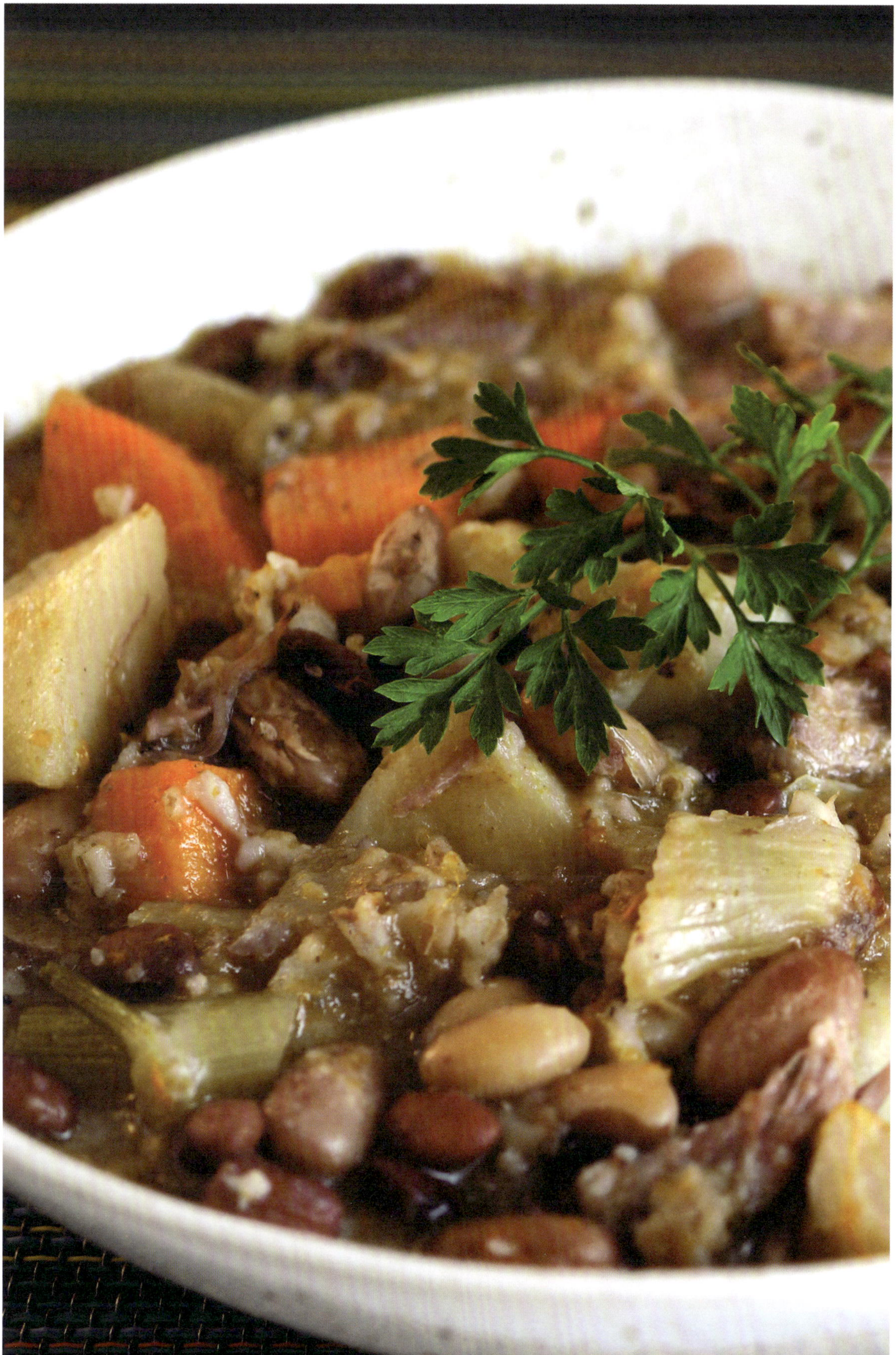

Samkeh Harra
(Fish with Spicy Sauce)

GF

Make your Shabbat table or your Succot spread extra beautiful with Samkeh Harra, a Lebanese fish dish full of flavor and a nice spicy kick. The Harra sauce is great on any fish but in particular with nice white flaky fish like Red Snapper, Porgy/Scup or even Halibut. Be sure to serve extra sauce on the side to make sure everyone gets enough!

Serves 4

INGREDIENTS

FOR HARRA SAUCE

Make the sauce first so you will have it ready to go when the fish comes off the grill or out of the broiler

2 tbsp olive oil

1 red onion, peeled & finely chopped

2 cloves garlic, peeled & minced

1 green Thai chile, finely chopped

2 red peppers, cored and finely chopped

1 large fresh tomato (about 1 cup), finely chopped

1 tsp coriander powder

2 tsp salt

½ tsp white pepper

2 tbsp cilantro, roughly chopped

2 tbsp fresh parsley, roughly chopped

¼ cup tahini

½ -1 cup water to thin out sauce to desired consistency

FOR THE FISH

2 lbs whole fish or 1-½ pounds of fillets (2 porgy or scup or 1 red snapper are good choices)

juice of 2 lemons + extra wedges for garnish

¼ cup olive oil

1 tsp salt

2 tsp cumin

1 tsp white pepper

INSTRUCTIONS

MAKE THE SAUCE

Heat a large cast iron pan, add olive oil and sauté onion on medium-low until onions are slightly translucent

Add garlic, chile and the spices to the pan and cook for a minute or so

Turn stove up to medium heat and add the chopped peppers and tomatoes to the pan. Cook for 2-4 minutes until peppers are soft

Stir in fresh cilantro, parsley and tahini

Add water for desired consistency

Taste and adjust seasoning if necessary

COOK THE FISH AND PLATE WITH SAUCE

Brush fish with olive oil, squeeze lemon juice all over and season with spices

Grill or broil smaller fish like scup 4-5 minutes each side and larger fish like snapper, 8-10 minutes each side

Move cooked fish to a platter and spoon Harra Sauce over the fish

Garnish with lemon slices and sprigs of parsley

NOTES

You can make the sauce ahead of time and just reheat it when you cook the fish.

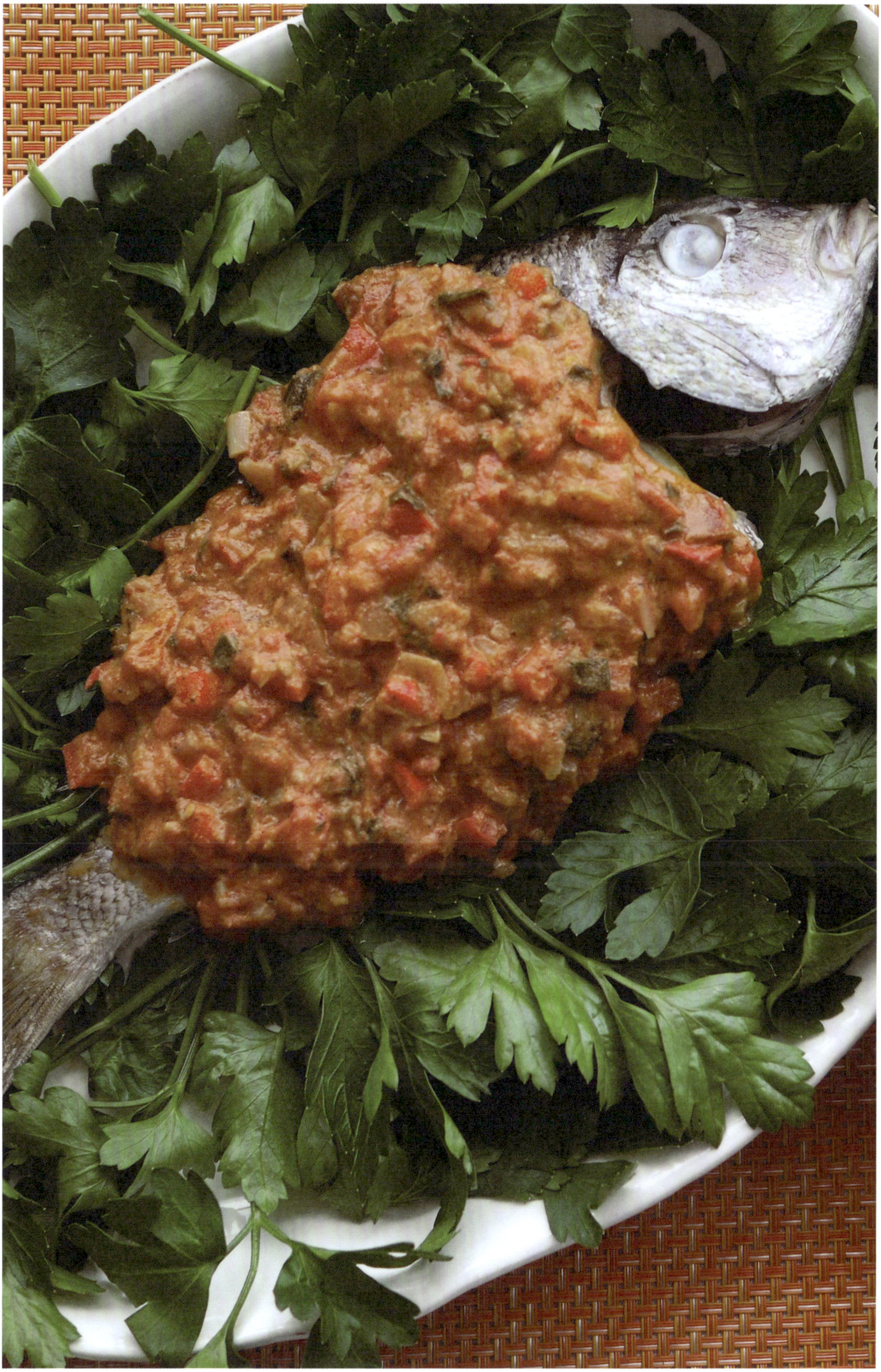

Falafel Wraps with Coconut Yogurt Sauce

V, GF

Falafel is such a delicious treat! We've developed a BAKED Falafel recipe that is guilt and gluten-free. Chia seeds are the secret of this recipe. They hold all the ingredients together without the use of any flour, eggs or other ingredients. It's magic!

Serves 8-10

INGREDIENTS

FOR FALAFEL

¾ cup chia seeds

2-¼ cups water

½ cup raw pistachios

½ cup raw almonds

½ cup ground raw flax seeds

½ cup sunflower seeds

½ cup sesame seeds

2 carrots, peeled & roughly chopped

½ onion, peeled & finely chopped

1 clove garlic, peeled & minced

2 tbsp extra virgin olive oil

1 tbsp parsley, finely chopped

2 tbsp nutritional yeast

juice of 1 lemon

1 tbsp cumin

salt & pepper to taste

FOR PLATING

2 cucumbers, peeled & chopped

3 heads of Boston Bibb or Butter lettuce, washed & dried

3 large heirloom tomatoes, finely chopped

1 large red onion, peeled & finely chopped

2 cups coconut yogurt

fresh dill

salt & pepper to taste

INSTRUCTIONS

MAKE THE FALAFEL

Pour 2-¼ cups water over ¾ cup chia seeds in a bowl, stir well and refrigerate for 10-15 minutes until chia absorbs the water and expands

In a food processor, pulse the almonds and pistachios into very small bits (you want to ensure the pieces are about as small or smaller than the whole sunflower and sesame seeds so they don't fall out once you combine them into the Falafel mixture)

Empty the food processor and add in the carrots. Pulse until carrot pieces are very small

In a large bowl, combine the soaked chia seeds with the ground flax seeds, pulsed nuts, pulsed carrots, whole sunflower seeds and the rest of the ingredients

Give the mixture a taste to ensure it's seasoned to your liking

Let the mixture sit in the refrigerator for 1 hour to overnight to give the ingredients time to solidify for easy shaping of the falafel balls

Once mixture is firm, make ping pong sized falafel balls (we use a small cookie dough scoop) and bake on a parchment-lined cookie sheet at 300°F for 1 hour

MAKE THE COCONUT YOGURT DIPPING SAUCE

INGREDIENTS

2 cups coconut yogurt (suggest a coconut yogurt with a thick consistency)

a handful of fresh dill, finely chopped

salt & pepper to taste

INSTRUCTIONS

Simply combine the ingredients and adjust seasoning as needed

PLATING

Serve about 3 falafel per person in a lettuce cup with fresh chopped cucumber, red onion and tomatoes (lightly salted) and topped with a dollop of the Coconut Yogurt Dipping Sauce

NOTES

You can form the Falafel balls ahead, freeze them and bake them later. Freeze the balls on a cookie sheet and then store them in zip-top bags in the freezer. To cook, bake straight from the freezer for about 1 hour, 10 minutes.

Stuffed Portobello Mushrooms

V, GF

If you want a "meaty" dish without the meat, these portobello mushrooms will surely satisfy. Enjoy an umami extravaganza! The fresh thyme brightens the dish and adds a hint of color along with the red peppers.

Serves 8-10

INGREDIENTS

2 tbsp coconut oil for cooking

1 tbsp coconut oil to mix with garlic purée to coat portobello mushrooms

1 cup shallots, peeled & finely chopped

3 cloves garlic, peeled & minced

1 additional garlic clove, peeled & mashed with 1 tbsp olive oil for coating portobello mushrooms (as mentioned above)

8-10 large portobello mushrooms, wiped clean and gills removed (to fit the stuffing)

1 cup of dried porcini mushrooms, reconstituted in hot water, drained & finely chopped

4 cups mixed mushrooms, wiped clean & finely chopped (we used shiitake, cremini and Hen of the Woods mushrooms)

1 red pepper, seeds and veins removed & finely chopped

1 chile pepper, finely chopped (remove seeds if you don't want spicy)

½ cup vegetable stock

2 tbsp coconut aminos (or gluten-free soy sauce)

juice of ½ lemon

salt & pepper to taste

2 tbsp fresh thyme, stems removed & finely chopped (plus extra for garnish)

INSTRUCTIONS

Preheat oven to 375°F

Rub the mashed garlic and olive oil all over portobello mushrooms and set aside. Or, if you want a bit of a smoky flavor, grill the mushrooms for about 1 minute each side

In sauté pan, cook shallots in coconut oil on medium-low heat until transparent

Add garlic and sauté for 1 minute

Add peppers and mushrooms and sauté 2-3 minutes

Add vegetable stock, coconut aminos and lemon juice

Season to taste with salt and pepper

Cook on medium heat until liquid evaporates, 3-5 minutes

Take off heat and stir in fresh thyme and adjust seasoning if necessary

Spoon mushroom mixture into the portobello mushrooms and bake 10-15 minutes

Serve with fresh dried thyme leaves sprinkled on top

NOTES

You can make the stuffing ahead of time and store in airtight containers in the refrigerator for 2-3 days before making the Stuffed Portobello Mushrooms.

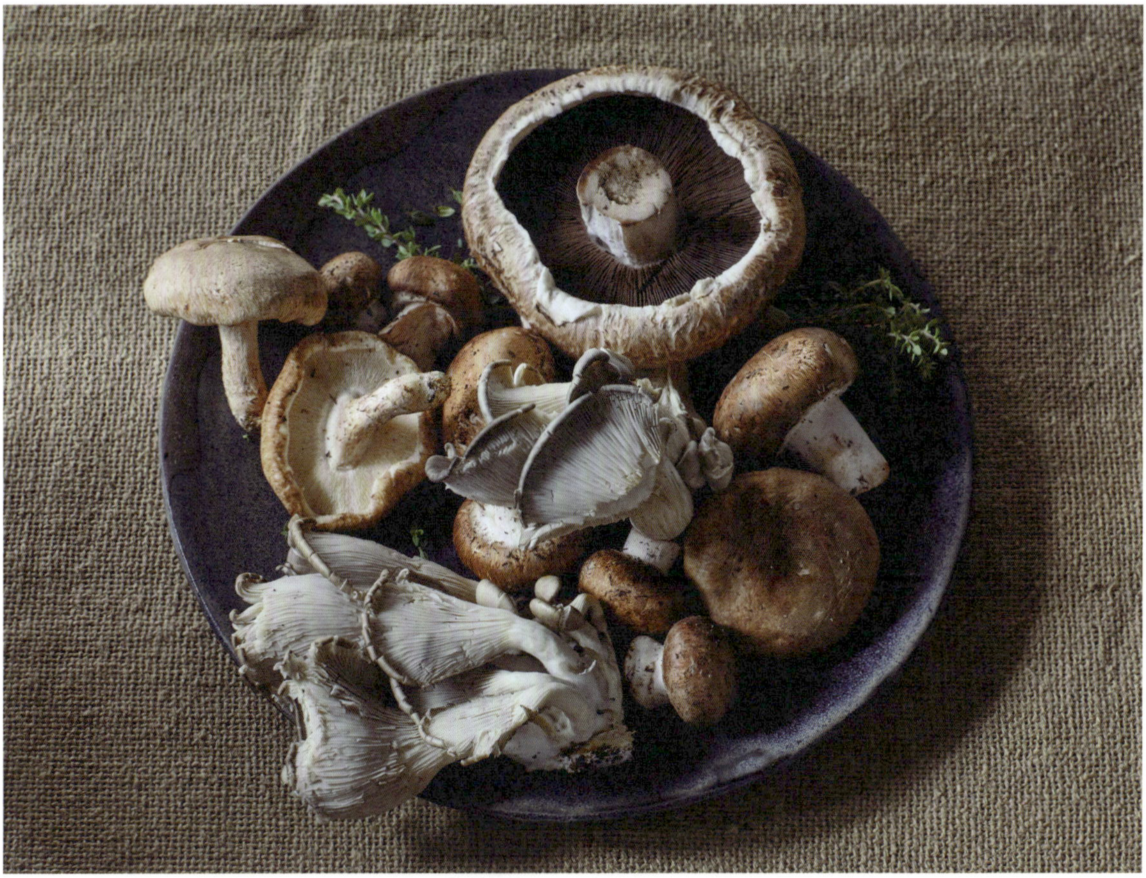

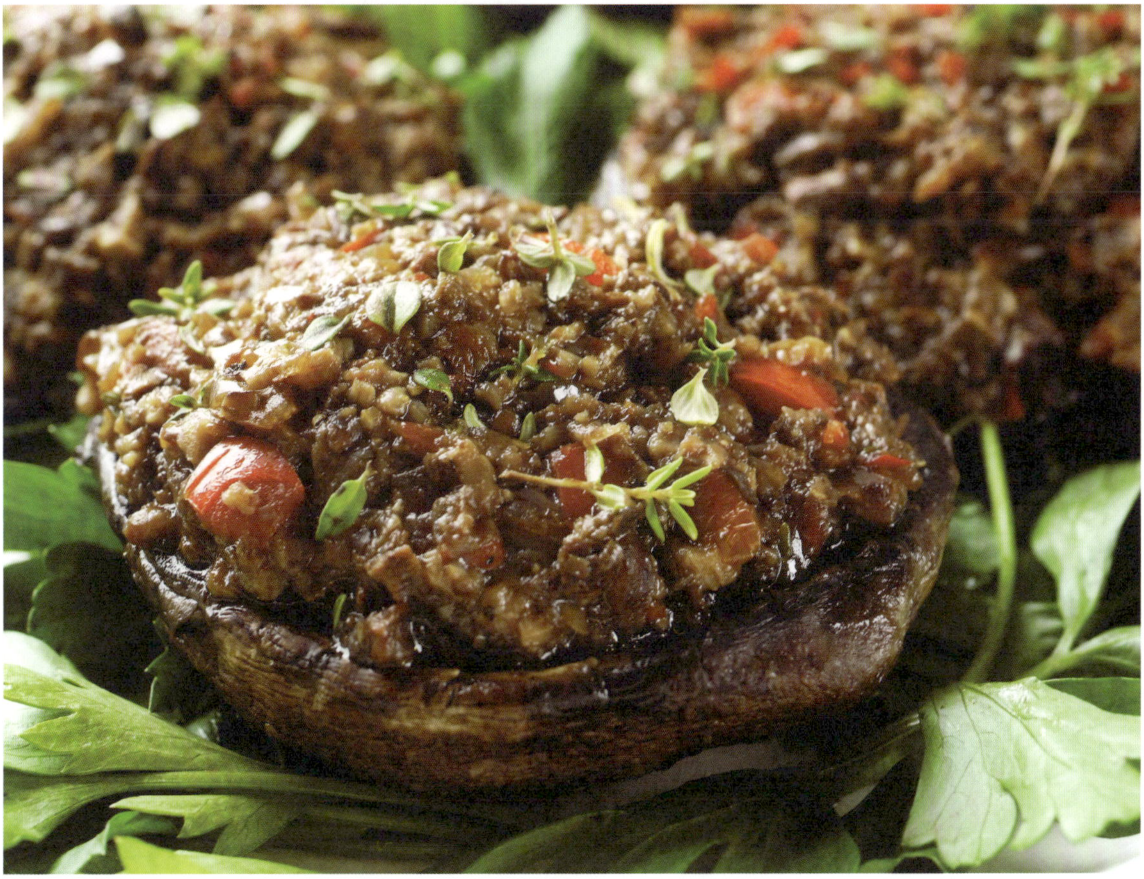

Chocolate Challah Bread Pudding

Challah is the delicious braided bread we eat on Shabbat each week, and since each year Hanukkah includes at least one Shabbat dinner, we love to make this bread pudding with our leftover challah. This is also a great dessert to include on your Bar/Bat Mitzvah menu! Because, who can resist chocolate!

Serves 12-14

INGREDIENTS

8 cups challah bread (crust removed and torn into bite-size pieces) — we used fresh bread but day-old bread is fine as well

4 cups milk

4 eggs

4 tbsp unsalted butter, melted

1 tbsp vanilla

½ cup sugar

1 tbsp cinnamon

1 tsp allspice

pinch of salt

¾ cup chocolate chips (bittersweet or milk chocolate) + extra melted chocolate for drizzling on top of plated slices

¼ cup cocoa powder

½ cup chopped walnuts (optional)

EQUIPMENT

9"x13" (3-quart) baking dish

INSTRUCTIONS

Beat eggs lightly in a bowl and set aside

Heat milk to scalding

Slowly pour milk into eggs whisking constantly so you don't curdle the eggs

Stir in melted butter, sugar, cocoa powder, vanilla and salt

Spread bread pieces evenly on bottom of dish

Sprinkle in chocolate chips

Pour milk and egg mixture over the bread and chocolate

Bake for 40 minutes at 350°F

Slice and serve with a drizzle of melted chocolate, scoop of vanilla ice cream or confectioners sugar and some fresh fruit

NOTES

The bread pudding will rise really high in the baking dish. Don't worry. it will settle once you take it out of the oven and let it cool.

SHABBAT

Etrog-Tahini Cookies

GF

A great post-Succot snack, these gluten-free cookies highlight the zest and juice of the etrog as well as the deep nutty sesame flavor of tahini. Very easy to make and you can chill the cookie dough days ahead and keep covered in the refrigerator until you're ready to bake.

Makes about 18 cookies depending on size

INGREDIENTS

½ cup almond flour

½ cup oat flour (or buckwheat or sorghum flour)

½ tsp baking soda

½ cup tahini (stir it well in the jar so it's not too watery)

zest of 1 etrog

2 tbsp etrog juice (if you don't have a juicer, it may be difficult to juice your etrog and you can use lemon juice instead)

½ cup raw honey

1 tsp vanilla extract

pinch of kosher salt

about 2 cups sesame seeds to roll the cookie dough in (mix of black and white sesame seeds is visually appealing)

INSTRUCTIONS

In one medium size bowl, mix the flours, salt and baking soda

In another medium size bowl, combine the tahini, honey, vanilla extract, etrog juice and zest

Pour the wet ingredients into the dry ingredients and stir until all ingredients are well blended

Chill for 30 minutes (or up to 3 days) covered in the refrigerator

When ready to bake, preheat oven to 325°F and line cookie sheets with parchment paper

Pour a generous amount of sesame seeds onto a plate

Scoop out about 1-½ tbsp of dough at a time, form into a ball and roll in the plate of sesame seeds until completely covered

Place your rolled balls on the cookie sheet and flatten with your fingers into a nice round cookie about ¼" thick (leave about 2 inches between each cookie on the sheet to allow a small amount of spreading while baking)

Bake your cookies for 8-9 minutes just until they get slightly brown on the sides (they don't need to be browned on top)

Let cool for a couple minutes before removing from cookie sheet and serving

Store the cookies in an airtight container or bag in the refrigerator for best results (if there's humidity in the air they may soften too much at room temperature)

SHABBAT

Apple-Cinnamon Parfaits

Simmering apples and cinnamon on the stove fills the kitchen with wonderful aromas. Not a grain of sugar or sweetener is added to this dessert and you won't miss it. The natural sweetness of the apples and blueberries are more than enough to satisfy any sweet tooth.

V, GF

Serves 8

INGREDIENTS

10 apples (Granny Smith, honey crisp or your favorite variety), peeled, cored & roughly chopped

fresh blueberries

plain or vanilla unsweetened coconut yogurt

cinnamon

chopped pistachios

½ cup water

INSTRUCTIONS

Place apples and ½ cup water in a stockpot with a heavy bottom and cook on medium-low heat until the apples soften to your liking — about 20 minutes

Layer your trifles. Start with a thin layer of coconut yogurt on the bottom, two rows of fresh blueberries, a generous layer of cooked apple, a few more blueberries and a dollop of coconut yogurt with cinnamon and a few chopped pistachios

NOTES

You can cook the apples ahead of time and keep in the refrigerator for 3-5 days.

SHABBAT

Mint and Rose Water Lemonade

V, GF

We go the extra mile with fresh lemons and mint to make this Lebanese-inspired lemonade special. We recommend having a pitcher on hand for Succot, Rosh Hashanah, Shabbat or any day you want a thirst quenching beverage to share that's a little out of the ordinary yet familiar and nostalgic.

Makes 6 cups

INGREDIENTS

FOR MINT & LEMON SIMPLE SYRUP

- 2 cups sugar
- 2 cups water
- 1 cup fresh mint
- 1 lemon, washed well & sliced

FOR LEMONADE

- 1 cup Mint & Lemon Simple Syrup (from above)
- ½ cup fresh mint
- 1 lemon, washed well, ends sliced off & seeds removed (keep skin on)
- ¼ cup rose water
- 1 cup ice
- 1 cup filtered water

INSTRUCTIONS

MAKE MINT & LEMON SIMPLE SYRUP

- In a saucepan, combine 2 cups water & 2 cups sugar
- Simmer over low heat until water has dissolved
- Remove from heat, add slices of 1 lemon and mint leaves. Cover pan and let steep for 30 minutes
- Strain out mint and lemons and pour simple syrup into a glass container
- Refrigerate

MAKE LEMONADE

- Blend all ingredients at high speed
- Strain liquid and serve in a pitcher with more ice or refrigerate

NOTES

You can make the simple syrup ahead of time and keep it chilled in the refrigerator for about a month. Add a little vodka for a pitcher of refreshing cocktails.

Food grade rose water can be purchased on Amazon or in specialty stores.

SHABBAT

Candles, Kiddush and Wine: Beginning and Ending Shabbat with Intention and Blessing

How do we begin and end sacred experiences? How do we carry a sense of the holy into everyday life?

Among the core religious practices of Judaism is the weekly celebration of Shabbat, the Sabbath. Rabbi Abraham Joshua Heschel, referred to the Sabbath as a "Palace in Time" — a day of rest, reflection and reconnection. In our contemporary age, when so much of life moves so quickly, Shabbat comes every Friday at sunset and beckons us to pause from our work-a-day routines and celebrate the essential gifts of life.

Since many Bar/Bat Mitzvah celebrations take place on Shabbat, we have included the following post about the rituals that help to usher in and bid farewell to the Sabbath. Often, the bar or bat mitzvah (and/or relatives) will be invited to lead one or more of these brief ceremonial acts in the synagogue or at home during the weekend festivities.

Candle Lighting (Hadlakat Neirot)

It is customary to welcome the Sabbath on Friday evening before sunset with the lighting of candles. Some people light two candles, representing different references to Shabbat in the two versions of the Ten Commandments in Exodus 20:8 (shamor, "keep" or "guard" the Sabbath) and Deuteronomy 5:12 (zakhor, "remember" the Sabbath). Others light one candle for each member of their family. Traditionally, this mitzvah was carried out by women whenever possible, but today this varies throughout the Jewish world. When lighting the candles, we symbolically step away from our ongoing efforts to create, build and master, recognizing and enjoying all that the Creator and Master of the Universe has provided for us. Candle Lighting is also used to initiate other major Jewish festivals.

Kiddush (Blessing over Wine)

On Shabbat and other festive occasions one begins the meal by reciting a blessing over a cup of wine or grape juice — a sign of bounty. Kiddush (literally "Sanctification") also refers to a modest repast held on Shabbat or holiday mornings after the communal prayer service. The text of the Friday evening kiddush speaks of the Sabbath as a "memorial" both to the creation of the world and to the exodus of the ancient Israelites from Egyptian bondage. In so doing, we give thanks to God for the great gifts of life and liberty.

Ha'Motzi (Blessing over Bread)

It is customary to follow the kiddush for Shabbat with a blessing over two loaves of bread. The two loaves represent the biblical teaching that the Israelites received a double portion of manna each Friday so that they did not have to labor for their food on the Sabbath (Exodus 16:4-30). The loaves are covered during the kiddush and unveiled when one is ready to recite the blessing over the bread (many people also ritually wash their hands before the ha'motzi). This assures that we focus on the meaning of each blessing and the sanctity of the moment. After reciting the ha'motzi blessing, it is customary to cut or tear one of the loaves (challah or challot [plural form]), dip the pieces in salt (as was done with sacrifices in the Temple) and distribute it to everyone partaking of the special meal to follow.

Havdalah (Service of "Separation")

Just as we welcome Shabbat with candle lighting and begin the Friday evening meal with kiddush, so too do we close the Sabbath with a brief ceremony that includes wine and a candle, as well as spices. The wine serves to sanctify the moment, the spices to revive our spirits as we bid farewell to Shabbat and the flame to call us back to our creative work in the world. Havdalah traditionally takes place when one has viewed three stars in the night sky, roughly an hour or so after sunset.

Scan for video

SHABBAT

Shabbat Discussion Questions

1. **HOLY:** Why is the first thing in the Bible which is called "Holy", Shabbat?

   Nothing created in the first six days of creation is called Holy. Even human beings. Of all God's Creations, only Shabbat is called Holy.

   How have you experienced the holiness in the Sabbath?

2. Shabbat literally means "to stop or to cease." In the six days of creation from Day 1 through the end of Day 6 nothing is declared Kadosh-holy.

   Why isn't anything that is created in the first six days of creation called holy?

   Why is the first that is called holy Shabbat?

3. **SET APART:** Why is it that time, specifically stopping in time, is the first thing that is set apart for God?

   Quick reminder: Kadosh-Holy means something set apart for God.

   What have you set apart in your life to create meaning and spiritual connection? Is there a special place you visit? Or a family routine that is sacred in your life?

4. **REST:** Shabbat is a Day of Rest and Kedusha/Sanctity. Is it enough to "rest" and "refrain" from doing activities on Shabbat? Suppose you do nothing all Shabbat — just eat and sleep. Have you celebrated Shabbat?

   Genesis 2:3 says "God blessed the seventh day, and made it holy." And the Ten Commandments tell us "to keep it [Shabbat] holy."

   How can we live in Shabbat? How can we feel holiness on Shabbat?

5. **STARTING TO STOP:** How do you prepare to stop on Shabbat?

   The experience of stopping for Shabbat is not like screeching to a stop at a red traffic light. You need to prepare to stop. Truly experiencing the holiness of Shabbat requires preparation and planning to allow for your sacred time and space of Shabbat.

How have you prepared to stop? What do you need to do in advance so that you can truly do nothing?

6. **SHABBAT IN THE MODERN WORLD:** Do we need Shabbat any longer, when we have weekends and days off? Does the Biblical calendar of Shabbat still resonate meaning in our modern, always-connected life?

What activities might you consider NOT doing on Shabbat in the modern world? Would not doing them restrict you or "liberate" you? Is there value to making this a routine part of your life? What would you do to make it special? What about a traditional Shabbat appeals to you? What might you add?

7. **SHABBAT IN ISRAEL**

Have you spent Shabbat in Israel? Have you ever experienced Shabbat in Jerusalem? How was it different? How did being in Jerusalem enhance the holiness of Shabbat?

8. **FOOD ON SHABBAT:** Food is very important on Shabbat and we are expected to have three meals.

Are there foods that are special for you on Shabbat? Would you feel right eating them any day of the week? Besides the food, is there something you would especially want for the Shabbat dinner table?

THE PASSOVER TABLE
NEW JEWISH TABLE
PASSOVER
One Hundred
Entertaining
D
I

DIY FUN PROJECTS 213

Apple Votives

Add some ambiance inside your succah, to your Bar/Bat Mitzvah tables, or any room in the house with these DIY Apple Votives. With all the hundreds of different heirloom apples ripe for the picking in the fall, you can create an array of colorful votives.

When you shop for your apples, choose ones that will sit flat on a table on its bottom. Any color or size is fine so let your creativity run wild. Take caution should you use real candles. You can purchase LED lights that work just like the real thing!

MATERIALS

12 apples

a permanent marker

tea lights or LED lights

matches

lemon juice

How to

STEP 1

Trace a tea light on top of apple with a permanent marker

STEP 2

Use a sharp paring knife to carve out the circle just deep enough to fit either a tea light or LED light. Make sure hole is deep enough to fit in tea light. Use the tea light to push into the center of the apple while carving. Prevent oxidation by dipping your cut apples in lemon juice or sprinkling them lightly with salt. This will prevent them from browning

STEP 3

Slide tea light or LED inside for a beautiful addition to your table

Scan for video

DIY FUN PROJECTS

215

DIY Seder Plate

Your kids will have a great time creating their own personal Seder Plate. Have them make it ahead of time so they can proudly display it on your Passover table.

Six traditional items are arranged on the seder plate, which is the focal point of the Passover Table. These include Maror (Bitter Herbs), Charoset (Mortar), Karpas (a vegetable), Zeroah (Lamb Shank), Beitzah (hard boiled egg), Chazeret (more bitter herbs). Each item has a special place on the seder plate, and each has a special significance to the retelling of the story of the exodus from Egypt.

Typically, seder plates are round with room for the word or image "Pesach" in the middle. Using a rectangle seder plate, you can create a non-traditional and modern seder plate with a spot for each of the 6 items. This is so simple to do! Make sure you date the bottom of the plate so this timeless piece can be used and remembered for many years to come.

MATERIALS

Serving Platter

Rectangle ceramic plates can be purchased at any home store…we found ours at Target. Just make sure it is large enough to hold all the seder items and bowls if you wish. Use small bowls or espresso saucers.

Sharpie oil-based markers (fine point)

Here's another version we made with small plates that fit into a larger tray. Use your imagination when you choose your dishes to make your seder plate.

How to

STEP 1

Wipe down paintable area with alcohol pad. Check out our templates here to use as a reference, or create or find your own pattern

STEP 2

Paint words and or images on bowls/plates or directly on plate. Outline first with black oil Sharpie and use alcohol swab with a cotton swab to remove excess paint. Then use Sharpies to color in images and decorate seder plate with all the items that appear on the plate for your Passover seder

STEP 3

Let paint dry for 24-48 hours

Scan for video

DIY FUN PROJECTS

217

How to Make Your Own Menorah

Menorahs are meaningful to each and every Jewish family. Whether they have been passed down through generations or new to the family, they are treasured. Creating a one of a kind Menorah for your family is a wonderful gift that your family can cherish for years to come.

It's fun and easy for kids to make their own Menorah. Menorahs can be made with items you may already have around the house.

MATERIALS

one 12" 2x4 or scrap wood

nuts (hardware) for making candle holders

sandpaper

clear glue or glue gun

Sharpie pen

paint (acrylic) or spray paint

glass mosaic pieces or other creative décor pieces for your Menorah

And if you want to make the candles for your Menorah, it's surprisingly very easy. To learn how, watch our Homemade Beeswax Candles video.

How to

STEP 1

Sand and paint a 2×4 and use a ruler to make 9 equally spaced marks across wood to indicate where you will be gluing the nuts

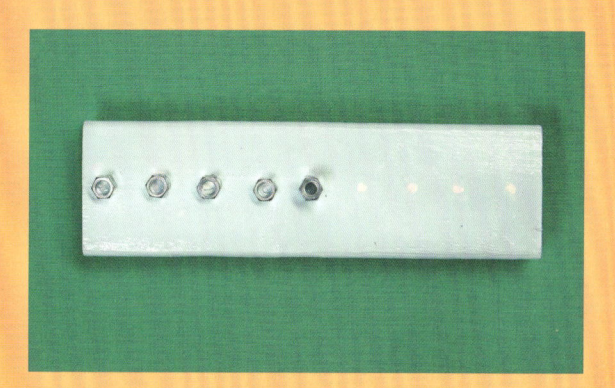

STEP 2

Glue nuts to Menorah with clear glue or glue gun so you won't see the glue. The middle candle holder (Shamash) should be raised, so stack two nuts on top of one another and glue together for this middle candle

STEP 3

Glue mosaic tiles (or your décor of choice) on top and sides of Menorah, fitting different sizes and shapes into place until the Menorah is completly covered

STEP 4

Light Menorah for 8 nights to celebrate Hanukkah! Please never leave burning candles unattended.

Scan for video

DIY FUN PROJECTS

Shibori Challah Cover

Shibori is the Japanese word for "twist or wring." This Japanese form of dyeing uses indigo as the main form of dye. Methods include dyeing fabric by rolling, bending, tying, binding, folding, twisting and pressing. We immediately fell in love with this form of dyeing as its main color is Indigo Blue. This technique originated in Japan (where Andy Goldfarb has lived and traveled throughout the years). One of the tricks behind indigo dyeing is that once you have prepared the bath of dye in your vat, it no longer appears blue until, of course, it is exposed to oxygen. Magic! Remember whatever you use to resist the fabric will repel the dye — be it wood, rocks and rubber bands. The materials used to resist can easily be found around your home. There are so many techniques from simple to abstract to create different patterns — we played around but look at our results!

Make sure to use a large enough napkin to cover the traditional two challahs on your Bar/Bat Mitzvah blessing table or your Shabbat table.

MATERIALS

Indigo Tie Dye Kit (available on Amazon and in craft stores)

napkins (for cover)

rubber gloves

5 gallon plastic bucket with lid

paint stirrer or yardstick for stirring

rocks or pebbles, rubber bands, wood boards, popsicle sticks

DIY FUN PROJECTS

Shibori Challah Cover
How to

STEP 1

Pour 4 gallons of warm water into bucket

STEP 2

Pour indigo powder into bucket. Stir in a circular motion

STEP 3

Pour soda ash and hydro from the kit into bucket while still stirring

STEP 4

Stir all contents slowly reversing opposite direction, dragging stick along wall of bucket to incorporate. Put lid on bucket and let rest 1 hour

STEP 5

While waiting for dye bath, start folding napkins! There are many techniques

You can use wood boards, rubber bands, binder clips, and rocks and wrap napkins in all different ways to find your favorite pattern. Here we used wood boards and rubber bands (both come with the Indigo Dye Kit). Have fun, try a variety of methods and make your original shibori design

STEP 6

Check back with dye after 1 hour to make sure the dye "flowers" on top

Move flower aside along the side of the bucket and make sure the dye is yellowish green — dye will not appear blue until it is exposed to oxygen

STEP 7

Dip items into "bath" for 10 minutes. We used wire to help hold items (you don't want them to hit the bottom of the bucket as it will pick up settled residue

STEP 8

Take Items out of bath (they will look green) and expose to air until it turns blue. Put lid on vat while you wait for items to change color

STEP 9

Unwrap items you dyed and run under water until water runs clear

Re-dip into dye another 5-10 minutes Let rest 12-24 hrs

Unwrap the rubber bands and boards and check out your design!! Make sure to wash out with water until it runs clear of dye

Voila!

Scan for video

DIY FUN PROJECTS

Additional Video Resources

PASSOVER

The Story of Charoset

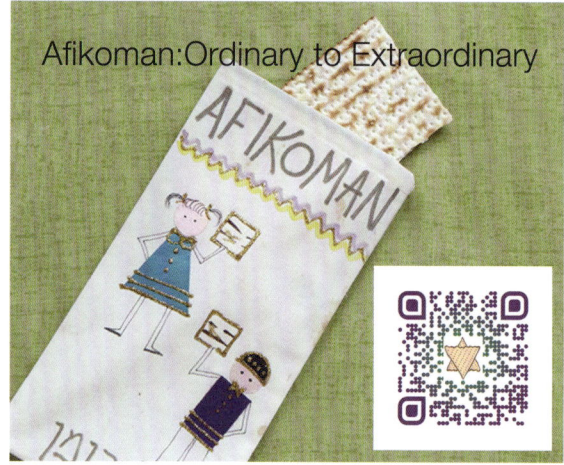

Afikoman: Ordinary to Extraordinary

SUCCOT

What is Succot?

The Succah Dance

HANUKKAH

Why We Light the Menorah

Lightning Fast Hanukkah

For more how-to and educational videos, please visit BreakingMatzo.com

Scan codes for video

PASSOVER

The History of Gefilte Fish

Passover: Spring Cleaning for the Soul

SUCCOT

Origami Apples

Apple Stamping

HANUKKAH

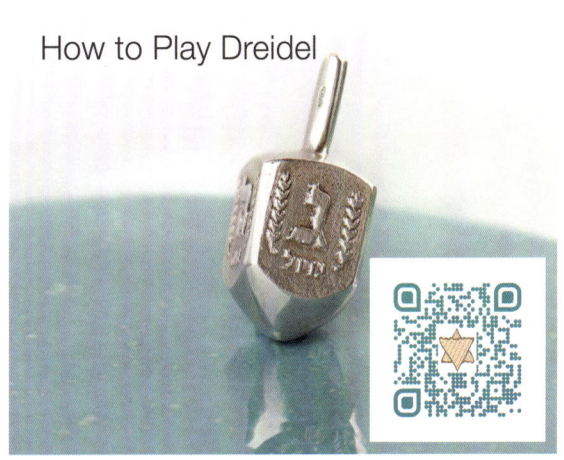

Homemade Beeswax Candles

How to Play Dreidel

ADDITIONAL VIDEOS 225

Jennie & Max Fish (Andy's Great Grandparents)

Acknowledgments

I am incredibly grateful to my family and friends for inspiring and teaching me about Judaism and Jewish cooking to make this book possible.

I would like to start with my great grandfather, Max Fish (11/28/1882-3/11/1974). Max Fish led my earliest Seder recollection. We celebrated Passover with the Fish / Goldfarb family in my early childhood.

I would like to thank my Mom and Dad for raising me in such an engaged Jewish home that valued learning and celebrated cooking.

I am indebted to my brothers, Laurence and Alex, who have carried on our cooking traditions and sharing of Jewish holidays.

I am grateful to my uncle Rabbi Daniel Goldfarb who teaches me Torah during my visits to Jerusalem and has contributed insights to Breaking Matzo.

Breaking Matzo would not be possible without our amazing team. Lynne Viera creatively executed my dreams and recipes and helped manifest Breaking Matzo. Kim Feinstein has expertly managed our digital content and amplified our social media presence. Thanks to Elisabeth Accardi for helping our family with so many fun celebration ideas. I would like to thank Jen Shockley for bringing Breaking Matzo alive on the pages of this book.

A special thank you to Valeria Brito who has helped our family with all of our Jewish Holiday celebrations. Valeria has beautifully activated my vision for Magic in every holiday.

I am deeply indebted to Rabbi Alan Ullman for opening my mind and connecting my heart with the Torah. Your spiritual guidance has provided the foundation of knowledge and spirit to Breaking Matzo.

Most importantly, I would like to thank my daughters, Caroline and Lucy, who have given me my reason to be on this planet. I love being your dad and sharing our incredibly magical Jewish holiday celebrations. Cooking and celebrating with you both has given me a lifetime of happiness and gratitude. I hope that you will both carry on our family spirit of Jewish celebration.

Andy with daughters Caroline (left) and Lucy (right)

About the Author

Andy Goldfarb believes in making life Magical, Meaningful and Memorable. As a father, Andy is dedicated to creating magical memory moments for his daughters in celebrating Jewish holidays.

Andy is passionate about food and loves cooking for his family and friends — Jewish classics taught by his mom (of blessed memory) as well as studying new recipes as he travels around the globe. In 2015, Andy founded Breaking Matzo to share his ideas of Food, Fun and Philosophy for making Jewish Home Holidays even more magical, meaningful and memorable. Andy believes that connecting favorite recipes, with philosophical underpinnings, while having fun for all generations during Jewish holiday celebrations, is critical. Andy hopes that this book, "Magical, Meaningful, Memorable" will help stimulate your mind, touch your heart and uplift your soul!

Recipe Index

V = Vegan   **GF** = Gluten Free

Almonds
- Charoset, Chinese, p. 16
- Charoset, Italian, p. 20
- Charoset, Piedmontese, p. 24
- Charoset, Spanish Sephardic (V)(GF), p. 26
- Charoset, Yemenite, p. 28
- Marzipan Stuffed Dates, p. 134
- Rose Water Almond Cookies (GF), p. 52

Apples
- Apple Cider Hot Toddy, p. 118
- Apple-Cinnamon Dessert Latkes, p. 161
- Apple Honey Cake, p. 110
- Apple Rose Pastries, p. 114
- Charoset, Classic Ashkenazi, p. 15
- Caroline's Apple Sauce (V)(GF), p. 137
- Apple-Cinnamon Parfaits (V)(GF), p. 204
- Parsnip and Apple Soup (V)(GF), p. 93

Artichokes
- Ground Beef and Thyme Stuffed Baby Artichokes (GF), p. 82
- Moroccan Inspired Vegan Stuffed Artichokes (V)(GF), p. 107

Beef
- Andy's Meat Sauce (GF), p. 138
- Bubbie's Stuffed Cabbage (GF), p. 142
- Classic Beef Meatballs, p. 146
- Grandma Boody's Brisket, p. 46
- Ground Beef and Thyme Stuffed Baby Artichokes (GF), p. 82
- Lebanese 7-Spice Kibbeh, p. 178
- Slow Cooker Short Rib Cholent, p. 193

Bourekas
- Potato-Leek, p. 174
- Spinach and Feta, p. 176

Bread
- Challah, p. 186
- Chocolate Challah Bread Pudding, p. 200
- Pita Bread, p. 188

Bulgur
- Lebanese 7-Spice Kibbeh, p. 178
- Tabbouleh (V), p. 96

Cabbage
- Bubbie's Stuffed Cabbage (GF), p. 142

Carrots
- Shang and Emma's Tzimmes (V)(GF), p. 35

Cashews
- Cashew Dipping Sauce (V)(GF), p. 85
- Charoset, Indian (V)(GF), p. 18

Cauliflower
- Cauliflower Mash (V)(GF), p. 149

Charosets
- Ashkenazi, Classic, p. 15
- Chinese, p. 16
- Indian, p. 18
- Iraqi (V)(GF), p. 18
- Italian (V)(GF), p. 20
- Moroccan, p. 22
- Piedmontese, p. 24
- Spanish Sephardic (V)(GF), p. 26
- Yemenite, p. 28

Cheese
- Classic Cheese Blintzes, p. 76
- Louisa's Kugel, p. 156
- Potato and Cheddar Latkes with Horseradish Sour Cream, p. 129

Chestnuts
- Charoset, Piedmontese, p. 24

Chia
- Falafel Wraps with Coconut Yogurt Sauce (V)(GF), p. 196

Chicken
- Charoset Chicken Salad, p. 32
- Chopped Liver (Gehakteh Leber) (GF), p. 182
- Golden Chicken Soup (Goldena Yoich) (GF), p. 43
- Schmaltz and Gribenes (GF), p. 40
- Za'atar Roast Chicken (GF), p. 140

Chickpeas
- Roasted Garlic Hummus (V)(GF), p. 87

Chocolate
- Chocolate Challah Bread Pudding, p. 200
- Chocolate Covered Matzo, p. 56
- Chocolate Matzo Mousse Cake, p. 54
- Gelt, p. 163
- Vegan Chocolate Pudding (V)(GF), p. 164

Coconut
  Coconut Cheesecake with Candied Lemon Curls (GF), p. 60
  Coconut Yogurt Sauce (for Falafel Wraps) (V)(GF), p. 196

Dates
  Charoset, Chinese, p. 16
  Charoset, Iraqi (V)(GF), p. 18
  Charoset, Moroccan, p. 22
  Charoset, Yemenite, p. 28
  Marzipan Stuffed Dates, p. 134

Donuts
  Loukoumades (Greek Sephardic Donuts), p. 154
  Sufganiyot (Jelly Donuts), p. 152

Eggplant
  Baba Ganoush (V)(GF), p. 88

Eggs
  Classic Cheese Blintzes, p. 76
  Nana's Puff Pancakes, p. 159
  Shakshuka (GF), p. 100

Etrog
  Etrog Marmalade (V)(GF), p. 30
  Etrog-Tahini Cookies (GF), p. 202

Figs
  Fig and Olive Tapenade (V)(GF), p. 190

Fish
  Chraime (Sephardic Fish Dish) (GF), p. 144
  Samkeh Harra (Fish with Spicy Sauce) (GF), p. 194

Gnomes
  Everywhere
  Anywhere

Grains
  Barley - Slow Cooker Short Rib Cholent, p. 192
  Bulgur Wheat - Lebanese 7-Spice Kibbeh, p. 178
  Bulgur Wheat - Tabbouleh (V), p. 96

Lamb
  Freedom Lamb, p. 48
  Kafta (Lebanese Lamb Kebabs) (GF) p. 80
  Sephardic Lamb Meatballs with Cashew Dipping Sauce (GF), p. 85

Latkes
  Apple-Cinnamon (Dessert), p. 161
  Potato, p. 126
  Potato and Cheddar with Horseradish Sour Cream, p. 129
  Sweet Potato, p. 130
  Zucchini, Gluten-Free (GF), p. 132

Legumes
  Lentil Curry over Cauliflower Mash (V)(GF), p. 149
  Slow Cooker Short Rib Cholent (with Beans), p. 192

Lemon
  Candied Lemon Curls, (Coconut Cheesecake garnish) (V)(GF), p. 60
  Mint and Rose Water Lemonade (V)(GF), p. 206

Love
  Essential Ingredient
  All Recipes Made with Love

Matzo
  Chocolate Covered Matzo, p. 56
  Golden Chicken Soup (Matzo Ball), p. 43
  Lucky Matzo Balls, p. 38
  Matzo Brei, p. 50
  Chocolate Matzo Mousse Cake, p. 54

Mom
  In Heaven
  With Us Always

Mushrooms
  Stuffed Portobello Mushrooms (V)(GF), p. 198

Nana
  In Heaven
  With Us Always

Olives
  Fig and Olive Tapenade (V)(GF), p. 190

Papaya
  Charoset, Indian (V)(GF), p. 18

Parsley
  Israeli Salad with Za'atar Dressing (V)(GF), p. 180
  Tabbouleh (V), p. 96

Pasta
  Butternut Squash Lasagna, p. 103
  Louisa's Kugel, p. 156

Pears
  Charoset, Spanish Sephardic (V)(GF), p. 26
  Vanilla and Anise Poached Pears (V)(GF), p. 116

INDEX

Recipe Index

Potatoes
    Potato and Cheddar Latkes with Horseradish Sour Cream, p. 129
    Potato Latkes, p. 126
    Potato-Leek Bourekas, p. 174

Puff Pastry
    Potato-Leek Bourekas, p. 174
    Spinach and Feta Bourekas, p. 176

Rose Water
    Mint and Rose Water Lemonade (V)(GF), p. 206
    Rose Water Almond Cookies (GF), p. 52

Salads
    Fattoush Salad (V), p. 94
    Israeli Salad with Za'atar Dressing (V)(GF), p. 180
    Tabbouleh (V), p. 96

Spinach
    Spinach and Feta Bourekas, p. 176

Squash
    Butternut Squash Lasagna, p. 103
    Butternut Squash Soup (V)(GF), p. 90
    Gluten-Free Zucchini Latkes (GF), p. 132
    Quinoa and Vegetable Stuffed Acorn Squash (V)(GF), p. 104
    Spaghetti Squash with Basil and Kale Pesto (V)(GF), p. 108

Sweet Potatoes
    Sweet Potato Latkes, p. 130
    Shang and Emma's Tzimmes (V)(GF), p. 35

Tahini
    Etrog-Tahini Cookies, p. 202
    Tahini Sauce (V)(GF), p. 190

Tomatoes
    Andy's Meat Sauce (GF), p. 138
    Israeli Salad with Za'atar Dressing (V)(GF), p. 180
    Shakshuka (GF), p. 100

Wine
    Chocolate Matzo Mousse Cake, p. 54
    Indian-Jewish Sangria (V), p. 62

Menu Index

PASSOVER MENU

Appetizers:
- Chopped Liver (Gehakteh Leber) (GF), p. 182
- Shang and Emma's Tzimmes (V)(GF), p. 35

Entrees:
- Freedom Lamb, p. 48
- Golden Chicken Soup (GF), p. 43
- "Lucky" Matzo Balls, p. 38
- Grandma Boody's Brisket, p. 46

Sides:
- Classic Ashkenazi Charoset, p. 15
- Moroccan Charoset, p. 22

Desserts:
- Chocolate Matzo Mousse Cake, p. 54
- Coconut Cheesecake with Candied Lemon Curls (GF), p. 60

Beverage:
- Indian-Jewish Sangria (V), p. 62

SUCCOT MENU

Appetizers:
- Kafta (Lebanese Lamb Kebabs) (GF), p. 80
- Ground Beef and Thyme Stuffed Baby Artichokes (GF), p. 82
- Sephardic Lamb Meatballs with Kosher Cashew Dipping Sauce (GF), p. 85

Entrees:
- Quinoa and Vegetable Stuffed Acorn Squash (V)(GF), p. 104
- Moroccan Inspired Vegan Stuffed Artichokes (V)(GF), p. 107
- Spaghetti Squash with Basil and Kale Pesto (V)(GF), p. 108

Sides:
- Fattoush Salad (V), p. 94
- Tabbouleh (V), p. 96

Desserts:
- Apple Honey Cake, p. 110
- Vanilla and Anise Poached Pears (V)(GF), p. 116

Beverage:
- Apple Cider Hot Toddy, p. 118

HANUKKAH MENU

Appetizers:
- Potato and Cheddar Latkes with Horseradish Sour Cream, p. 129
- Sweet Potato Latkes, p. 130
- Gluten-Free Zucchini Latkes (GF), p. 132

Entrees:
- Za'atar Roast Chicken (GF), p. 140
- Bubbie's Stuffed Cabbage (GF), p. 142
- Chraime, p. 144

Sides:
- Caroline's Apple Sauce (V)(GF), p. 137
- Lentil Curry Over Cauliflower Mash (V)(GF), p. 149

Desserts:
- Sufganiyot, p. 152
- Louisa's Kugel, p. 156

Beverage:
- Indian-Jewish Sangria (V), p. 62

SHABBAT MENU

Appetizers:
- Chopped Liver (Gehakteh Leber) (GF), p. 182
- Potato-Leek Bourekas, p. 174

Entrees:
- Slow Cooker Short Rib Cholent (GF), p. 192
- Samkeh Harra (Fish with Spicy Sauce) (GF), p. 194
- Stuffed Portobello Mushrooms (V)(GF), p. 198

Sides:
- Challah, p. 186
- Homemade Pita, p. 188

Desserts:
- Chocolate Challah Bread Pudding, p. 200
- Etrog-Tahini Cookies (GF), p. 202

Beverage:
- Mint and Rose Water Lemonade (V)(GF), p. 206

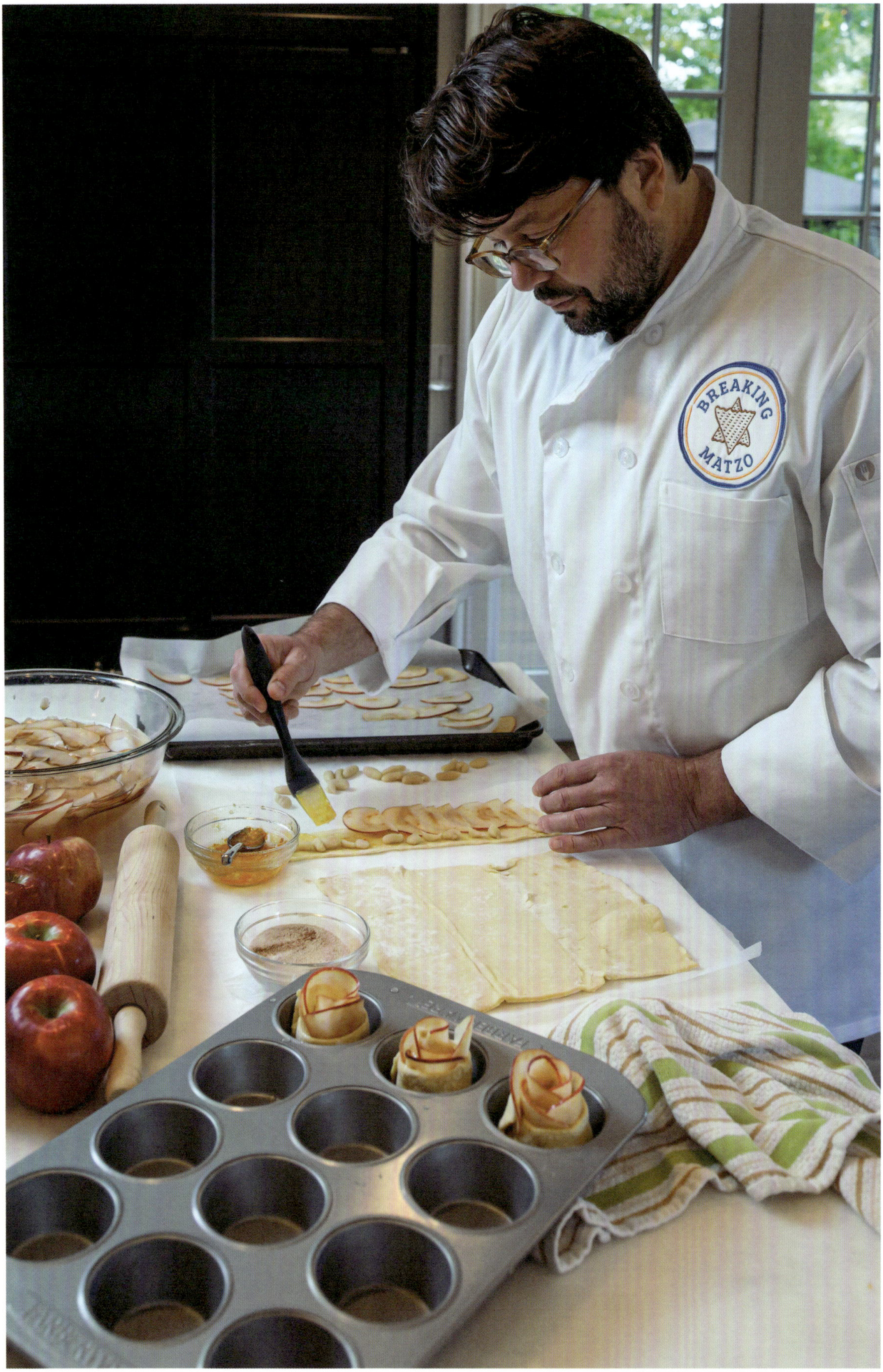
BREAKING
MATZO

Copyright © 2019 Andrew P. Goldfarb

All rights reserved. No part of this publication may be reproduced, distributed, or transmitted in any form or by any means, including photocopying, recording, or other electronic or mechanical methods, without the prior written permission of Andrew P. Goldfarb.

Andrew P. Goldfarb
One Boston Place
Suite 2810
Boston, MA 02108

ISBN: 978-0-578-61124-2

Cover photograph by Quentin Bacon. Book design by Jennifer Shockley.
Photographs by Quentin Bacon appear on pages 36-37, 42 (*raw vegetables*), 51 (*matzo stack*), 98-99, 101, 124-125, 139, 170-171, 199, 209, inside back cover.
Photographs by Nina Gallant appear on pages 15, 17, 19 (*Indian Charoset*), 21, 22, 25, 27 (*Spanish Sephardic Charoset*), 33, 40-41, 42 (*Golden Chicken Soup*), 44-45, 49, 51 (*Matzo Brei*), 52-53, 55 (*Matzo Mousse Cake*), 57, 63, 66-67, 77, 84, 95, 102, 112-113, 115, 127, 128, 131, 133, 136-137, 141, 143, 145, 147, 150-151, 153, 155, 157, 158-159, 160, 163, 167, 168-169, 183, 201, 212-213, 218-219, 224-225 (*The Story of Charoset; Afikoman: Ordinary to Extraordinary; Why We Light the Menorah; Lighting Fast Hanukkah; Homemade Beeswax Candles; How to Play Dreidel*).
Photographs by Joe Murphy appear on pages 4-5, 10 (*Lucy; Andy & brothers in Breaking Matzo aprons*), 12-13, 46, 78-79, 121 (*dining table inside Succah*), 226 (*Andy & family standing at Passover*), 229, 234.
Photographs by Jessica Delaney Photography appear on pages 122-123, 214-215, 224-225 (*What is Succot?; Origami Apples; Apple Stamping*).
Photographs by Connor Linde appear on pages 68-69, 216-217.
Photograph on pages 210-211 by Fred Braunstein Photography.
Photograph on pages 64-64 by Myra Yellin Goldfarb Outwater.
Photographs on pages 19 (*Iraqi Charoset*), 30-31 (*etrogs in boxes; Etrog Marmalade*), 59 (*candied lemon spirals; Coconut Cheesecake with Candied Lemon Curls*), 81, 83, 86, 89, 91, 92, 97, 105, 106, 109, 111, 117, 119 (*Apple Cider Hot Toddy*), 135, 148, 165 (*Vegan Chocolate Pudding*), 173, 177, 179, 181, 189, 191, 193, 195, 197, 199 (*Stuffed Portobello Mushrooms*), 203 (*kids & Rabbi with etrogs in Brooklyn; Etrog-Tahini Cookies*), 205, 207 courtesy of Breaking Matzo, LLC.
Photographs on pages 2, 8, 10 (*Caroline, Lucy, & Andy's mom; camel riding; childhood Succot; Andy & family vintage*), 30 (*Andy & daughters*), 34; 42 (*Andy & his mom*), 55 (*Caroline making the dessert*), 75, 121 (*Succah 1973*), 224 (*The Succah Dance*), 226 (*Jennie & Max Fish; Andy & daughters in desert*) courtesy of the author.
Supplemental photographs are used under official license from Shutterstock.com.

Recipes that contain nuts should be avoided by those with a known allergic reaction to nuts and nut derivatives. Raw or lightly cooked eggs should be avoided by pregnant women, the elderly and young children. Recipes designated as vegetarian, vegan and/or gluten-free are the opinion of the author and are not intended to be statements of vegetarian, vegan, or gluten status. Please review product labels.

Printed and bound in the United States
First Edition

Scan to visit BreakingMatzo.com